Brian Jones
The Original Rolling Stone

Astrology, Beliefs, Health & Psychic Sensitivity

ANDREA J MILES

GREEN MAGIC

Brian Jones. The Original Rolling Stone
© 2024 by Andrea J Miles. All rights reserved.
No part of this book may be used or reproduced in any
form without written permission of the author, except
in the case of quotations in articles and reviews.

Green Magic
53 Brooks Road
Street
Somerset
BA16 0PP
England
www.greenmagicpublishing.com

ISBN 978 1 915580 19 1

Designed and typeset by Carrigboy, Wells, UK
www.carrigboy.co.uk

GREEN MAGIC

Brian Jones in the garden at Cotchford Farm (1969).
Wikiimedia Creative Commons: CCBY-SA-30.
Gift from Jones's parents. Unknown author.

Brian Jones
1942–1969

Multi-instrumentalist, vocalist, founder & original leader of the Rolling Stones.

'Such psychic weaklings has Western civilisation made of so many of us'.

Brian Jones

DEDICATION

This book is dedicated to Brian Jones and to all those who loved and love him.

THANKS TO

Dawn Young for encouragement of the book.

Kevin Rowan-Drewitt for proof-reading and suggestions.

Mark Hetherington for technical support with astrological charts.

Kathy Rowan, Sarah Dowding, Marilyn Stroud and Valerie Daines for being there all throughout the process of this project, for listening and supporting me.

Contents

PART ONE

The Story of Lewis Brian Hopkin Jones   11

PART TWO

What Brian Jones's Natal Chart Reveals and the
    Astrology in Action   45

PART THREE

Natal & Transit Charts   129

ILLUSTRATIONS

Fig. 1. Brian Jones natal chart & the transits to it
    when he died.   134
Fig. 2. Brian Jones natal chart & the transits to it
    when his sister Pamela died.   135
Fig. 3. Anita Pallenberg's natal chart.   136
Fig. 4. Jimmy Page's natal chart.   137

PART ONE

The Story of Lewis Brian Hopkin Jones

Brian Jones was born Lewis Brian Hopkin Jones during the middle of the Second World War on Saturday 28th February 1942 in Cheltenham, Gloucestershire and was of Welsh descent. His father was Lewis Blount Jones who was born on 3rd September 1917 and died in September 2009. Jones's mother Louisa Beatrice Jones was born in October 1918 and died in 2011. Jones's paternal grandparents were both teachers from Pencoed near Bridgend.

Lewis Blount Jones studied at Leeds University where he gained a BSc degree in engineering. He married Louisa Beatrice Simmonds in Wales in 1938. Her father was a master builder and also an organist at a church near Cardiff. In 1939 the newly married couple moved to Rosemead, Eldorado Road in Cheltenham (Wyman & Havers, 2002, 10).

Mrs Jones taught the piano and her husband became an aeronautical engineer with the Dowty Group manufacturers which was a global engineering group (www.dowtyheritage.org.uk) and he remained in their employment until the early nineteen-eighties (Facebook/Dowty Group of Companies). He shared his wife's interest in music and was able to play the piano and the organ. Mr Jones also taught the piano as well as leading the choir at the local church in Cheltenham.

At the age of four Jones had an attack of croup which left him prone to bronchitis and asthma, the latter a chronic affliction which plagued him as a boy and then in adulthood it developed into a more nervous asthma which was induced at moments of high stress. Mr and Mrs Jones's two other children were Pamela who sadly died from leukaemia in 1945 aged two and Barbara their second daughter was born in 1946. When Mrs Jones's son was six years old, she started to teach her son how to play the piano (theory and sight reading). He continued to learn with his mother until he was fourteen years old (Wyman & Havers, 2002, 16).

In September 1949, Jones was enrolled at the fee-paying Dean Close Junior School in Cheltenham where the (then) bespectacled student excelled in English and Music. He passed his eleven-pus exam in July 1953 and then attended Pates Cheltenham Grammar School in September 1953. After his fourteenth birthday he became first clarinet in the school orchestra. Jones led a rebellion against the prefects while he was at the grammar school, and as a result of this he was suspended from school for a short while (Aftel, 1982, 21).

His headmaster at the Grammar School Doctor Bell claimed that *'Brian's father was forever turning up in my study, totally unannounced, with complaints. He was on Brian's back all the time. Brian was a clever boy, an intelligent rebel, introverted, withdrawn, but he wasn't a bad lad'* (Giuliano, 1994, 5). Clearly, the headmaster had insight as to the bigger picture, even though he had to punish Jones for leading the aforementioned rebellion.

When it came to sports Jones appeared to have no natural skill although he did enjoy badminton and diving (Wyman & Havers, 2002, 19) and often swam at the Cheltenham Lido. Although he was frequently in trouble at school and was regularly caned it did not stop him from achieving seven O-levels and continuing his education into the sixth form.

Whilst he was in the lower sixth year he obtained two further O-Levels and later A-Level chemistry and physics. Irrespective of Jones's lack of academic application his IQ of 135 would undoubtedly have aided him in passing his exams.

He apparently *'kept himself to himself when he was at school'* (Broomfield, 2023, Magnolia Pictures) so presumably was seen as a loner by some of the teachers and students. He did have some school friends though who remember him from those schooldays, for example Roger Limb and Graham Ride who spoke of their memories in a recent BBC Arena documentary *'The Stones and Brian Jones'*.

Jones's parents were disappointed with him when he quit education for they had aspirations for him to attend university and follow a profession. Jones was under no illusions that higher education was not for him stating *'I quite honestly didn't feel much of an urge to do anything else except play music. I thought about different jobs and rejected them: I knew I'd be bored stiff'* (Wyman& Havers, 2002, 23).

Indeed, he had a multitude of jobs which were short-lived which included working in Sid Tongs' record shop (Admin/Gloucester Nylon Spinners/Facebook Group), bus conductor, a junior architect, coalman and an ophthalmic assistant. Employment for Jones was straightforward enough to secure but maintaining work was less successful. Even after he had moved to London in the early nineteen-sixties, he occasionally returned to Cheltenham and sought work whilst he was there, one example being the position at Nylon Spinners.

Jones detested school, and the authority it represented, finding it conformist and regimented. He loathed school uniforms and having to have his hair cut short for school. His resentment to authority figures resulted in him being suspended from school on two occasions (Wyman & Havers, 2002, 19). One being the incident of him leading a rebellion against the prefects.

His father said that when his son reached his teenage years his *'rebellion was against parental and school authority'* (Broomfield, 2023, Magnolia Pictures). In his late twenties Jones expressed to his girlfriend Anna Wohlin how he *'started to revolt at an early age ... I saw that there was a lot wrong with our society and I enjoyed provoking people to see how far I could bend the rules which I thought were just too old-fashioned'* (Wohlin, 2005, 65).

In 1961 Jones applied for a scholarship at Cheltenham Art College, his application was successful. However, two days later the offer was withdrawn after somebody had written to the college informing them that Jones was *'irresponsible and a drifter'* (Wyman & Havers, 2002, 29).

It was evident from an early age that music was Jones's passion, he reflected *'Musically I was guided by my parents ... eventually I found I had a feel for music. I guess I knew that I was going to be interested only in music from very early on'* (Wyman & Havers, 2002, 15). When he was fifteen his parents bought him a saxophone which he was obsessed with for a short while. Two years later for his seventeenth birthday they bought him an acoustic guitar (Wyman & Havers, 2002, 23). Clearly, indeed encouraged his playing of musical instruments.

The teenaged Jones loved traditional jazz as well as sauntering around the Cheltenham coffee bars such as the Aztec, El Flamenco and the Patio. These haunts attracted avant-garde artists, musicians and social outcasts (Giuliano, 1994, 8). He also worked and spent recreational time at

Filby's Jazz Club in Cheltenham where they played Howlin' Wolf records (Broomfield, 2023, Magnolia Pictures). He began playing in bands and became a member of the 66 Club which was a local jazz event, although as we know Jones went on to become a blues purist.

Back in September of 1959 he went hitchhiking in Scandinavia with friends. Taking his guitar, he busked for a while until he was out of money and then returned to Cheltenham (Wyman& Havers, 2002, 28). Whilst he was in Scandinavia he indulged in his new found liberation *'mingling with bistro musicians and free thinking Bohemians as well as loving and leaving the willowy, willing Swedish women'* (Giuliano, 1994, 8).

The Cheltenham based band *The Ramrods* boast that they gave Jones his first break. Apparently, he had rehearsed and played saxophone with them prior to him meeting Ian Stewart before going on to form *The Rollin Stones* aged nineteen (www.wherecanwego.com/ and Facebook /The Ramrods @ Cheltenham).

Eventually Jones had to find alternative accommodation as the strained relationship between him and his parents became intolerable and he left the family home which by then was at 335 Hatherley Road. He and his friend Dick Hattrell along with two art students rented a large bedsit in Parabola Road, Cheltenham (Wyman & Havers, 2002, 28).

Before he went travelling aged just seventeen, Jones's schoolgirl girlfriend Valerie Corbett (also aged seventeen) became pregnant and it is believed he tried to persuade her to have a termination (Wyman & Havers, 2002, 23). However, she refused and carried the child until it was born in May 1960. She gave birth to a son and by this time the relationship between her and Jones had ended. Their child was given up for adoption which was usual in that era for young unmarried mothers.

In November 1959 Jones met a married woman called Angeline at a concert; it is believed the pair had a one-night stand which resulted in her pregnancy. A daughter, Belinda was born and raised by Angeline and her husband, apparently Jones never knew about the pregnancy or birth (Wyman & Havers, 2002, 28). In 1960 Jones started dating Pat Andrews; she became pregnant and in 1961 gave birth to their son Julian Mark Andrews (www.freebmd.org.uk) who is also known as Mark.

In early 1962 Andrews and their son moved into 102 Edith Grove, Chelsea which was a cold and squalid flat, especially the kitchen. Jones and Mick Jagger were already living there when Andrews and Mark moved in followed by Keith Richards who also became a tenant. Andrews worked hard to support herself, Mark and Jones. However, the strain of the situation became too much for her. Leaving a note for Jones she returned to Cheltenham with their son (Wyman & Havers, 2002, 38). Apparently, her actions affected him greatly; consequently, he lost his job and had a breakdown.

Not long after Andrews returned to her family, Jones's Cheltenham friend Dick Hattrell moved into the Edith Grove. He recalled how Jones sometimes treated his genuine friends appallingly and with derision. For example, Hattrell recalled how on one occasion *'It was snowing and he sent me out for some fags, then locked me out for the rest of the night ... He always wanted something new to happen'*. Food and money were in short supply and Hattrell's stay with his flatmates was short-lived, in addition he was in ill-health as he had a burst appendix and decided to moved back to Cheltenham (Wyman & Havers, 2002, 39).

His memory about Jones treating his loyal friends shockingly was echoed by Bill Wyman. He recalled how on one occasion the band were being interviewed on film and that Jones who was standing behind the seated Wyman, deliberately flicked cigarette ash into his hair without him knowing. He added in the recent Broomfield documentary that Jones *'was cruel sometimes'* and that after stubbing out a cigarette butt on Wyman's hand whilst they were in a car that Jones later said to him *'sorry man I didn't mean it'* (Broomfield, 2023, Magnolia Pictures). Yet, despite the malicious tactics he remains extremely loyal to Jones.

After his relationship with Pat Andrews dissolved, Jones began dating Linda Lawrence and in 1963 she gave birth to his fourth child Julian Brian Lawrence. Eventually, the relationship between Jones and Lawrence broke down. In 1970 she married Scottish folk pop singer Donovan Leitch and together they raised Julian and changed his surname to Leitch. Their son was named after a Jazz Sax hero of Jones called Julian 'Cannonball' Adderley.

In 1964 the parents of Dawn Molloy, who was also a girlfriend of Jones, informed him and the Rolling Stones management that their daughter was pregnant with his child. The group's then manager Andrew Loog Oldham gave Dawn Molloy a cheque for £700 and made her sign an agreement to say that the matter was closed and that she would not disclose to the media anything about Jones or their child (Young in email correspondence to author).

She was forced to give up their son Paul Andrew for adoption just as Valerie Corbett had given up their child up for adoption. Like so many other unmarried pregnant women in the early 1960s, Dawn Molloy was made to suffer in a society that forbade them a say in the fate of their children (Young, 2013, 268). However, in 1994 she was reunited with her son and continues to have a loving and thriving relationship with him (Young 2013: acknowledgment page). Jones also had a daughter, Barbara Anbna Marion whose mother is unknown in the public domain (www.classicbands.com). Possibly there are other children now adult whose father was Lewis Brian Hopkin Jones.

It is worth noting that contraception in England was not as accessible to younger and unmarried people in the nineteen fifties and nineteen sixties as it is now. Furthermore, G.P. services then were reluctant to engage in providing birth control advice or the supply of contraceptives. It was not until 1961 that the birth control pill became prescribed on the NHS. In addition by this time there was wider availability of more reliable latex condoms as well as the introduction of plastic intrauterine devices (www.peopleshistorynhs.org/).

In the mid-sixties during an interview Jones commented on the generation gap between a child and it's parents, explaining how that as a young child it is a reflection of their character. Then the child matures and forms its' own opinions and ideas and has a personality and that the parents feel like they have lost their child. He delivers the topic in a cool and logical manner (www.youtube.com) and surely his comments were autobiographical, drawing from his own childhood being raised in the nuclear family from which he rebelled.

For example, Jones stated '*A child is a thing to be loved. A child is the manifestation of both parents and both parents see themselves in the child. The child is part of them, he is their flesh and blood and for a good many years he is a reflection of their character*'.

He went on to say that once the child grows up and asserts their own personality that the parents no longer recognise themselves in his personality and feel they have lost him, when all that has happened is that he '*has become a human being in his own right*'. Clearly Jones was not referring to himself abandoning his illegitimate children. Instead reflecting upon his own experience of being raised by a mother and father.

Jones revealed in the last few months of his life to his girlfriend Anna Wohlin '*My most fervent wish is to be reunited with my sons Julian and Mark … I sometimes feel really guilty and I hope they'll give me a second chance to get to know them better*' (Wohlin, 2005, 65). This shows that he was capable of self-reflection and had emotionally matured acknowledging his responsibility towards his sons.

Wohlin recalled how he enjoyed entertaining the children of his friends John and Pamela Mayall when they all visited him at his country home Cotchford Farm, Hartfield, East Sussex in 1969. Jones was immensely proud of his property and it's gardens. It was a fifteenth century farmhouse and one of its' former owners was A.A. Milne author of the *Winnie-The-Pooh stories*, Jones purchased the property in 1968.

Whilst the Mayall family were visiting, he kept the children amused as they played in the swimming pool and where he entertained them with his skills. He leapt from the springboard and dived into the water imitating different animals which made the children howl with laughter and naturally Jones enjoyed the attention (Wohlin, 2005, 161).

In 1966 while Jones was on tour with the band, he met up again with German-Italian actress, model and artist Anita Pallenberg; they had met previously on another occasion and this time they became a couple. The earlier time they met was in Paris in 1965 when Pallenberg was with Prince Stash Klowosski de Rola (actor, entrepreneur, author music producer and singer). The latter at the time was a member of *Vince Taylor and The Playboys* band and *The Stones* were on the same bill. However, mythology surrounding the couple getting together, usually states that it was while *The Stones* were on tour in 1966 that Jones and Pallenberg *first* met (Prince Stash in conversation with the author).

After the 1966 tour Jones and Pallenberg began living together and their toxic relationship began. Jones frequently abused and violated her. Tom Keylock who provided security for Jones and the rest of the band noted *'Brian used to get pissed or stoned and he'd knock her about'* (Giuliano, 1994, 57). On one occasion when he arrived at Jones and Pallenberg's home, she told Keylock *'He gave me a good hiding … Look a black eye'*. Keylock told Jones *'Don't do that Brian. Anyone can hit a woman, that's not big. Do it again and I'll thump you'*. In another instance after punching her in the face, Jones broke his hand (www.rollingstone.com), his injury was not lost on his fans.

In September 1966 *Stones* fan Alan Powell saw the band play at the Empire Theatre in Liverpool. He remembered that as he sat at the rear in row 'V', he was able to see that Jones had his hand bandaged and played his dulcimer with a big white feather (Houghton, 2015, 260). Pallenberg finally left Jones in 1967and began a relationship with Keith Richards. She told music author and journalist Stanley Booth that Jones '*always hurt himself ... He was very fragile, and, if he ever tried to hurt me, he always wound up hurting himself*' (Wells, 2021, 66) which presumably would explain the aforementioned bandaged broken hand.

Other subsequent relationships that Jones had were with British fashion model Linda Keith, English model Suki Poitier (a favourite of fashion designer Ossie Clark) and Swedish model Anna Wohlin, as well as a brief affair with the world's African American cover girl Donyale Luna. Sadly, the latter died in 1970 from an accidental overdose (www.marieclaire.com). Previously in 1968 he had a relationship with French actress, model and singer Zouzou who found prominence after appearing in the film *Love in the Afternoon* by Eric Rohmer in which she played the lead role (www.en.wikipedia.org).

When Jones first moved to London in the early sixties, he became involved with musicians such as Jack Bruce, Paul Jones and Alexis Korner. Bruce went on to become bassist with the band Cream and Paul Jones went on to become the singer of the band Manfred Mann. Before these bands were formed Jack Bruce, Paul Jones and Alexis Korner were all involved with the small London rhythm and blues scene (www.en.wikipedia.org).

Korner and Cyril Davies formed the group Blues Inc Incorporated, Korner played electric guitar and Davies harmonica playing country blues. Together they established a residency at The Ealing Jazz Club, West London in 1961 (Wyman & Havers, 2002, 32). At that time Charlie Watts played on drums; Dave Stevens on piano, Dick Hestall-Smith on tenor sax and Andy Hoogenboom on bass for the Blues Incorporated.

Before Jones moved to London, he and Dick Hattrell hitchhiked from Cheltenham to Ealing so they could see Alexis Korner Blues Incorporated play their debut show. After the gig Jones gave Korner a tape that he and Paul Jones had made of their music. The two Jones's had formed a group called The Roosters. When Brian Jones left the group he was replaced by Eric Clapton (www.denofgeek.com).

Jones persuaded Korner to let him play with his band and in 1962 he played slide electric guitar with Blues Incorporated performing under the name *Elmo Lewis*. The name was a nod to one of his blues heroes Elmore James and Jones played *Dust My Broom* (Wyman& Havers, 2002, 33). He said *'I discovered Elmore James, and the earth seemed to shudder on its axis'* (Wyman & Havers, 2002, 31). Korner's wife Bobbie recalled how *'Brian was the most driven-special curious young man'* (Cooper & James, 2020, an appreciation Paul Trynka).

The title *Dust My Broom* was released by Elmore James in 1951 and was a rendition of Robert Johnson's *'I Believe I'll Dust My Broom'* which was recorded in 1936. Jones was also inspired by singers and songwriters: Chuck Berry, Jimmy Reed, Muddy Walters, Sonny Boy Williamson and Howlin' Wolf to name but a few.

In May 1962 Jones placed an advert in the *Jazz Weekly* which was a Soho club information sheet. His advert invited musicians to audition for a new R & B band at the Bricklayers Arms pub which then was on the corner of Broadwick Street (off Wardour Street) and Duck Lane in Soho.

THE STORY OF LEWIS BRIAN HOPKIN JONES

Pianist Ian Stewart was the first person to respond to the advert, shortly afterwards Mick Jagger and his childhood friend Keith Richards joined the band that Jones had formed. To begin with the group did not have a name but eventually they became *The Rollin' Stones* which was the name given by Jones and it was inspired by Muddy Walter's track *Rollin' Stone Blues* (www.en.wikipedia.org/). The letter 'g' at the end of *Rollin'* was added later.

In July 1962 the band played their first gig at the Marquee Club and at that time the group comprised of drummer Tony Chapman, Mick Jagger, Brian Jones, Keith Richards, Ian Stewart and bass player Dick Taylor, later of the band *The Pretty Things*. Other drummers had temporarily been in and out of the newly formed band and included not only Chapman, but also Mick Avory later of *The Kinks* and Ginger Baker later of *Cream* (Davis, 2002, 26).

At the end of 1962, once Charlie Watts had agreed to join *The Rollin' Stones*, Tony Chapman was fired at the Ricky Tick venue in Windsor. Jones told him '*Sorry, man but you have to fuck off*', understandably Chapman was angry (Davis, 2002, 40). Watts had a fine reputation from other musicians as being one of the better drummers in London and had already played with other bands, including, and as already noted, Alexis Korner's the Blues Incorporated and a blues band called *Blues by Six*.

A.E. Hotchner commented that when Jones '*left home and struck out on his own, he was determined, in fact driven, to succeed, and his belief and commitment carried the other tentative boys he had recruited-Mick Keith, Dick, Ian and Charlie-along with him*' (Hotchner, 1990, 374). This shows the faith that Jones had in himself as well as the band members having confidence in their (then) leader. A search for a permanent bass player remained and, eventually, Jones selected Bill Wyman who then was part of a band called *The Cliftons*.

From 1962 to 1963 after Pat Andrews had moved out from 102 Edith Grove (and later Dick Hattrell as previously noted) Jones shared the flat with Jagger and Richards and also a future photographer called James Phelge. The Nanker/Phelge writing credit was used for all early band compositions particularly the instrumentals. During that period Jones and Richards spent many hours listening to blues artists such as Jimmy Reed, Muddy Walters and Howlin' Wolf. During their tenancy at Edith Grove, Jones also taught Jagger how to play the harmonica.

While acting as *The Rollin' Stones* business manager at this time Jones paid himself an extra five pounds which caused great resentment from the other band members. His justification being that he was the person who was proactive in making the telephone calls and writing letters for bookings as well as replying to the vast amount of fan mail that they received (most of which was for Jones).

He considered himself the leader of the band and Jagger and Richards were incensed when they found out, particularly since music impresario Giorgio Gomelsky had become the band's 'de facto' manager, although it was never formalised by a signed contract (Dumaurier, 2023, 45). It was at the Marquee Club in 1962 that Gomelsky first met Jones and between approximately 1963 and 1964 he became involved with *The Rollin' Stones* (Dumaurier, 2023, 38).

THE STORY OF LEWIS BRIAN HOPKIN JONES

Jones's multi-instrumental ability was extraordinary and varied widely. He could play all the band's instruments which varied from bass, drums, guitars and piano. His ability to play a wide array of instruments is particularly apparent on the albums *Aftermath* (1966) *Between the Buttons* (1967) and also in 1967 *Their Satanic Majesties Request*.

In the earlier days of the band Jones's preference was to play a Vox white teardrop shaped electric guitar, He also played a range of acoustic and electric guitars from companies such as Gibson and Fender. Illustrations of Jones's slide guitar contributions can be heard on tracks such as *I Wanna Be Your Man, Little Red Rooster* and *No Expectations*. His rhythm-guitar style can be heard on tracks such as *19th Nervous Breakdown* and his guitar riff on *The Last Time*. Jones's grandson Joolz Jones (son of Julian Jones-later Leitch) said of his blood grandfather's playing that on *'No Expectations – his slide is absolutely beautiful'* (Cooper & James, 2020, Jones Ireland 2019).

The diversity of his genius musical ability is further evidenced by the following: – he played sitar on *Paint it Black* and *Street Fighting Man,* organ on *Let's Spend the Night Together,* marimba on *Under my Thumb* and *Out of Time,* recorder on *Ruby Tuesday,* saxophone on *Child of the Moon* and *Citadel,* kazoo on *Cool, Calm and Collected,* Appalachian dulcimer on *I am Waiting* and *Lady Jane,* meletron *She's A Rainbow, We Love You* and *2000 Light Years From Home*. On the track *Dandelion* he also played oboe/soprano sax (https://en.wikipedia.org/).

Jones can also be heard playing harmonica on many of the band's earlier tracks such as *Come On, I Just Want To Make*

Love To You and *Not Fade Away*. One fan commented having seen the band '*I was very impressed by the harp playing of Brian and also his pear-shaped guitar*' (Houghton, 2015, 181).

The volume of musical instruments that Jones would play in any one performance is evident by the memory of fan Sean Gleeson. He saw *The Rolling Stones* perform at the Savoy Theatre, Cork in 1965. He recalled '*Brian Jones playing his Vox teardrop guitar and his Vox amp. He also used two harmonicas during the show and played slide guitar*' (Houghton, 2015, 180).

He was also a backing vocalist right through until as late as 1968 when he sang on *Sympathy for The Devil*. His earlier track contributions as a backing vocalist include: *Bye Bye Johnny, Come On, It's All Over Now, I Can't Get No Satisfaction, I Wanna Be Your Man, Money, Poison Ivy* and *Walking the Dog*. On the latter track and as part of the song, his contribution includes whistling (as in whistling to a dog).

Jones and Keith Richards' guitar playing was distinctive and key to the sound of the band. Both played rhythm and lead although Jones played the slide guitar solos whilst Richards played the majority of the standard guitar solos. Fan Joe West recalled that when he saw the band play at the Odeon Theatre in Sunderland in 1964 how he '*… was blown away by the slide guitar of Brian Jones*' (Houghton, 2015, 85). Gleeson, the fan who saw them in Cork, continued with his memory stating that '*Keith Richards and Brian Jones swapping guitar parts on songs, Brian Jones playing slide and letting his guitar hang from his shoulders when he played harmonica*' (Houghton, 2015, 180).

Another fan, John Philpott was influenced by Jones and his harmonica playing when he saw the band perform in 1964 at the Granada Theatre, Rugby he claimed '*… what really struck* *me was Brian Jones's harmonica – I'd never heard blues harp before and it knocked me out so much that I went out the next day and bought a Hohner Vamper harmonica for ten shillings and sixpence (53p)'* (Houghton, 2015, 80).

Between the years 1963 and 1967 The Rolling Stones were managed by Andrew Loog Oldham and this was the beginning of the end of Jones's band as he knew it. Oldham was not interested in the band playing blues and cover versions anymore. He believed that in the long term this would not be financially sustainable for the band. He believed it would be lucrative if the band wrote their own songs and so delegated Mick Jagger and Keith Richards to the role of song writing. Although the pair wrote original songs many of them retained a bluesy sound.

In addition, Jagger was required by Oldham to make his captivating and showy performance fundamental to the band's live performances. He amplified his managerial power over the band which included the group being able to play fewer blues tracks. Ultimately, Jones recognised that his influence over the blues group which he founded, managed and named had diminished significantly.

The situation brings to mind some of the lyrics in *Ruby Tuesday*, those words being *'Lose your dreams and you might lose your mind. Ain't life unkind?'* Marianne Faithfull described *Ruby Tuesday* as Jones's *'swan song'* (www.christies.com/en/lot/lot-3902546); *The Stones* were his heart and soul. The exhaustion from the band's intense touring schedules, coupled with money and fame as well as feeling increasingly estranged from the band, largely resulted in Jones's overindulgence with alcohol and drugs. This excess led to the detriment of his mental and already weakened physical health.

In the latter part of the sixties Jones *'was flirting dangerously with an all-out depression'* (Jackson, 1992, 134), Ray Davies of *The Kinks* observed that when Jones was off-stage it seemed to him that Jones *'had difficulty coping with the real world … Brian also though seemed to have the additional problem of being slightly schizophrenic'*. Author Mandy Aftel concluded how Jones's *'manic-depressive behaviour'* had complicated a friendship that he had with a woman in the spring of 1968 (Aftel, 1982, 175). Irrespective of them enjoying each other's company his drastic mood swings proved too much for his friend to cope with. These examples from Davies and Aftel provide an indication as to how fragile Jones's mental health had become in the late nineteen sixties.

In April 1967 the German film *Mord und Totschlag* (English translation *A Degree of Murder*) was released. It starred Anita Pallenberg and was directed by Volker Schlöndorff, who was a German director, screenwriter and prominent member of the New German cinema of the late 1960s and early 1970s (www.en.wikipedia.org/).

The soundtrack was produced by Jones and the recording sessions for it took place during late 1966 and early 1967 at the IBC studios in London. Jones played on the soundtrack as did other established musicians such as the (then) *Yardbirds'* guitarist Jimmy Page and the (then) *Small Faces* drummer Kenny Jones. The film won three German film awards and was entered into the *Cannes Film Festival* (www.en.wikipedia.org/wiki) although it did not win.

When Anita Pallenberg left Jones in 1967 for Keith Richards the relationship between Jones and Richards became further strained. As tensions increased so did Jones's alcohol and substance abuse. His musical contributions lessened and increasingly he was absent from the band's recordings sessions.

In May 1967 Jones was arrested for drug possession and the authorities also found marijuana, cocaine and methamphetamine in his flat. Jones was arrested at his flat with his friend Prince Stash. The latter recalled how he was staying at his friends flat with him and how the telephone kept ringing with calls from whom they assumed were the press asking if they had *'been busted already'* (www.youtube.com/wondery). At first the friends were baffled as to what was going on, the calls were relentless and the pair came to the realisation that it was the police posing as the press trying to gain access into Jones's flat.

Eventually, approximately fifteen police officers gained access to the flat and announced they had a warrant to charge him. They went into Jones's bedroom and under the mattress bed found a purple and yellow Moroccan wallet, which had mouldy grass in it. Neither Jones nor Prince Stash had ever seen the holder before. The police also found in an abandoned trunk of Pallenberg's, a mouldy bottle of liquid methedrine, as well as an empty phial which had a couple of cocaine crystals in it.

In his autobiography *Bent Coppers,* Norman Pilcher (who arrested Jones) is described as *'the most infamous police officer in British law enforcement history'* (Pilcher, 2020, o/side back cover). He claimed *'We'd always get sent a lot of intelligence on Brian Jones … he mainly dealt with prescription drugs but he did other stuff too, on occasion'* (Pilcher, 2020, 47). Pilcher continued *'unbeknownst to the newspapers, it often transpired that we would end up in a friendly relationship with the people we arrested'* (Pilcher, 2020, 47).

Caroline Coon was arrested with Mick Jagger's brother Chris, at a protest in December 1967 called the *'Free Brian Jones'* march in the Kings Road, Chelsea. This was about the jail sentence of Jones because of drugs charges. Coon was released from prison on bail. She went on to form the Release charity which still exists today and is an independent and national charity. It is also the national centre of expertise on drugs and drugs law (www.release.org.uk/).

The following year on 21st May 1968 Jones was arrested again for being in possession of cannabis which was found in a rolled up ball of wool in a bureau in his flat. He was jailed on 31st October 1968 and spent one night at HM Prison Wormwood Scrubs and released on bail the following day for £2,000 (Giuliano, 1994, 215).

In June 1967 Jones attended the Monterey Pop Festival where he had been specifically invited by Jimi Hendrix to introduce *The Jimi Hendrix Experience* onto the stage (Mitchell & Platt, 1993, 50). *Hey Joe* was released in the Dec of 1966 and went to No 5 in UK but, sadly, failed to chart in USA. However, there was an auspicious phone call from one of the organisers of the festival, John Phillips of *The Mamas & The Pappas*.

The deal was that none of the artists would be paid but all expenses would be covered. *The Jimi Hendrix Experience* accepted the invitation on the condition they could take Jones along with them to introduce the band to the crowd. In 1968 *The Jimi Hendrix Experience* covered singer-songwriter Bob Dylan's *All Along the Watchtower* for their third studio album *Electric Ladyland*. Jones an avid fan of Bob Dylan, played percussion on *Watchtower* he used an instrument called a vibraslap (www.en.wikipedia.org/wiki).

The Jimi Hendrix Experience was often visited by other musicians dropping in on their recording sessions including Jones. Mitch Mitchell recalled that '*Jimi always had a very soft spot for Brian ... They'd see each other quite a lot ... Brian would go back to Jimi's place occasionally or vice versa*' (Mitchell/Platt, 1990, 81). Apparently, Hendrix also went to Morocco with Jones and their mutual friend Deering Howe (Mitchell/Platt, 132). Mitchell remembered that '*Jimi remained friends with Brian right up until Brian's death, which I think, hit Jimi really hard* (Mitchell/Platt, 1990, 83).

Jones became further alienated from *The Rolling Stones* and as resentment grew the opposition between him and Jagger and Richards was intensifying. Charlie Watts, Keith Richards Bill Wyman were all in agreement that Jones could be cruel and difficult, as well as friendly and outgoing.

In his autobiography *Stone Alone*, Bill Wyman said of his colleague '*There were at least two sides to Brian's personality. One Brian was introverted, shy, deep-thinking. The other was a preening peacock, gregarious, artistic, desperately needing assurance from his peers*' (Wyman & Coleman, 1997, 83). He continued that Jones '*pushed every friendship to the limit and way beyond*' (Wyman & Coleman, 1997, 45). According to Andrew Loog Oldham, Jones could at times be unfriendly and antisocial (www.en.wikipedia.org/wiki).

In 1968 Jones participated with *The Rolling Stones* in recording sessions. At this time the band were producing *Jumpin' Jack Flash* and the *Beggars Banquet* album. Jones can also be seen in the film *One Plus One* which was directed by Jean-Luc Goddard who rose to fame in the 1960s as pioneer of the French New Wave film movement.

The film records the making of *Sympathy for the Devil* which was written by Mick Jagger and Keith Richards and appears on side one track one of *Beggars Banquet*. In the film Jones can be seen playing acoustic guitar, chatting and sharing cigarettes with Richards although he is neglected in the music making.

In December 1968 Jones made his final appearance with *The Rolling Stones* in the film *The Rolling Stones Rock and Roll Circus* which the band organised, it was a part-concert, part circus-act film. It included other artists such as John Lennon, Jethro Tull and The Who.

Prince Stash was made infamous with his arrest along with Jones in the mid-sixties and recalled how excruciating it was for him to watch Jones in *Rock and Roll Circus* stating that *'Brian is a shadow of himself. He doesn't do any of the introductions properly. I'm just aghast when I see him on that. He can barely hold it together'* (Houghton, 2015, 271). Clearly, distressed about the disintegration of his friend he added *'Brian. This amazing force. This amazing beacon of light that he had been was a sorry caricature'*.

Marianne Faithfull recalled just how much Jones's demise was palpable in 1968 she wrote *'the angelic Brian vanished and, in its place, came this puffy Pan-like figure with a permanently stupefied grin on his face'* (Faithfull, 1994, 245).

Previously and whilst on probation during September of 1968, Jones was arrested again and found with possession of cannabis in his home which he claimed had been left by the previous tenants of his flat. As he was still on probation, he faced a hefty prison sentence if he was found guilty. The jury did find him guilty. However, the judge was sympathetic towards Jones and instead of sending him to prison fined him fifty pounds and instructed him *'For goodness sake, don't get into trouble again or it **really** will be serious'* (Wyman & Havers, 2002, 311).

Earlier in the summer of 1968 Jones recorded the Morocco-based ensemble the *Master Musicians of Joujouka (Jajouka)* which was posthumously released in 1971 as *'Brian Jones Presents the Pipes of Pan at Joujouka'*. The group are trance musicians who serve as a modern representation of a century's old music-tradition and played on instruments passed along from generation to generation for hundreds of years. *'It was Jones intention to learn how to play Joujouka music like the natives, and then adapt it to the Stones' recordings'* (Hotchner, 1990, 301).

Although Jones could not speak their language, he managed to convey to the musicians his desire to learn how to play (Jackson, 1992, 168) like them. This shows his determined nature at work and his love and respect for their music, as well as a passion to learn from them. Laura Jackson author of *Golden Stone* observed that Jones frequently said with complete frankness that *'there were musicians in the world who were playing better than him and would never be heard by a mass audience'*. It was his recordings which helped bring the Joujoukans to widespread international attention (www.en.wikipedia.org/wiki/). When Jones worked with the band and produced the album, the group was led by Hadj Abdesalam Attar; the *Master Musicians* are now led by Attar's son Bachir Attar.

Painter and author Mohamed Hamri (aka *Hamri*) was one of the few Moroccans to participate in the Tangier Beat Scene helped bring Jones to Jajouka in 1967. Hamri later paid homage to Jones by creating a painting called *Brian*

Jones Joujouka Very Stoned and which appeared on the *Master Musicians'* album cover *Jajouka Black Eyes* (www.en.wikipedia.org/wiki/Brian_Jones). In 1995 the album *Brian Jones Presents the Pipes of Pan at Jajouka* was re-released in co-operation with Bachir Attar and composer and pianist Philip Glass.

On the rare occasions when he did appear at recording sessions he provided little in terms of musical contributions and the band would switch off his amplifier which lead to Keith Richards playing almost all of the guitars (www.en.wikipedia.org/wiki.). Author Gary Herman wrote of Jones's demise that he was *'literally incapable of making music; when he tried to play harmonica his mouth started bleeding'* (Herman, 1982, 44).

His behaviour was challenging during the band's recording sessions for the studio albums *Their Satanic Majesties Request* and *Beggar's Banquet* and by the time they started recording *Let It Bleed*, Jones's general behaviour had significantly worsened. For example, in March of 1969 he borrowed the group's Jaguar abandoning the parked car to go shopping in the Pimlico Road. The police towed it away and Jones hired a chauffeur driven car to take him home (www.en.wikipedia.org/wiki). Just two months later he crashed his motorbike and had to be taken to hospital.

In 1969 *The Rolling Stones* wanted to tour the United States which would have been the first time in three years. However, the recent legal troubles with Jones made it even more challenging for the band to acquire a US work visa. That situation along with the estrangement from his bandmates, his addictions and frequent mood swings made him a liability and he was in no fit condition mentally or physically to tour with the band.

During May of 1969, he made two contributions to the work in progress: autoharp on *You Got The Silver* from the album *Let It Bleed* and percussion on *Midnight Rambler* from the same album. Also in May 1969, Mick Jagger gave Jones strict instructions that he must attend a photo shoot else he would be fired from the band. Appearing frail and weak Jones was present at the required photo shoot and the images appeared on the album *Through the Past, Darkly* (*Big Hits Vol 2.*) which was released in September 1969.

In June 1969, Jagger, Richards and Watts visited Jones at Cotchford Farm. On that visit on the 8th June the three band members told him that the group he had formed would continue without him (Wyman & Havers, 2002, 324–326). Jones was replaced by the twenty-year old Mick Taylor who had formerly been a member of *John Mayall's Bluebreakers*.

The story given to the public about Jones made it appear as if he had voluntarily left *The Rolling Stones*. Whilst the group had made it plain to him that he had been dismissed from the band they gave him the option of how he wanted to declare the news to the general public. The following day he made a statement announcing his departure from *The Rolling Stones*. He declared '*I no longer see eye-to-eye with the others over the discs we are cutting*' (Wyman & Havers, 2002, 326) indicating artistic differences as the reason why he left the band.

Leading up to the point of the eventual dismissal, Jones was visited at Cotchford Farm by musician friends such as Alexis Korner, John Mayall and Mitch Mitchell and he contacted others such as John Lennon about the new band he wanted to form. Apparently, in the weeks before his death he had demoed a few songs and two of the titles included *Has Anybody Seen My Baby* and *Chow Time* (www.en.wikipedia.

org/wiki). When Korner visited his friend, he observed that Jones seemed *'happier than he ever been'* (Wyman & Havers, 2002, 329).

However, when John Mayall and his family visited Jones, just two days before his death, they *'were shocked by how unwell he looked. He looked incredibly frail and had trouble walking: in fact, he seemed ready to fall over if he wasn't holding on to something'* (Mayall with McIver, 2019, 177).

Mayall observed that Jones *'was a shadow of his former self and looked and behaved like a little old man ... he was totally serious and excited about putting some new music together'*. Mayall experienced a terrible shock when he learnt that his friend was found dead in his swimming pool just two days after he and his family had visited Jones at his home (Mayall with McIver, 2019, 178).

Nearing midnight on the 2nd July 1969 Jones was discovered motionless at the bottom of his swimming pool. His then live-in girlfriend Anna Wohlin was sure that he was alive when he was taken out of the pool and insisted that he still had a pulse. By the time the doctors arrived it was too late and Jones was pronounced dead on arrival at the hospital.

The coroner's report stated that the injury or disease causing Jones's death was *'Ia) drowning, Ib) Immersion in fresh water, II) Severe liver dysfunction due to fatty degeneration and the ingestion of alcohol and drugs* (Giuliano, 1994, 252/253), as to *the death'* – *'Drowning whilst/under the influence of Alcohol and Drugs/<u>MISADVENTURE</u>'*. Copies of the death certificate were released to the press and the details therein, endorsed the scandal which took precedence over any accomplishments that Jones ever achieved in his lifetime. In 1994 Dr Cyril H. Wecht a prominent forensic pathologist examined the official documents related to Jones's death with reference to the scientific data contained in the records (see *Part 3/Fig. 1* in the transits explanatory text for further details).

Some fifty years later, Norman Pilcher had plenty to say in his autobiography about Jones's death. Upon hearing the news that Jones was dead he said that *'it was very sad, but worse than sad: a chain of events had just begun which was to cause confusion, bewilderment and secrecy of a dark nature throughout the force, and indeed the country'* (Pilcher, 2014, 47).

He continued that his interest in *Jones 'regarding drugs was over, but on a personal view I was intrigued in the circumstances surrounding his death, mainly because things didn't add up'* (Pilcher, 2014, 48). After a police investigation into his death the inquest recorded a verdict of Accidental Death. Pilcher's own view was *'that Jones had met a violent death and was in fact murdered ... I was convinced that Jones had been killed by his building contractor Frank Thorogood, to whom he owed considerable sums of money for work carried out by Thorogood ... I am convinced that this was a major cover up.*

Pilcher also believed that instead of a coroner's enquiry Jones's death should have been treated as *'a suspicious death enquiry, properly dealt with by the local CID and it never happened'* (Pilcher, 2014, 49). Reflecting upon Jones and his personality he said *'As unpleasant he was as a man, and as hated as he was by some, he was very talented and he did not deserve death.* Keith Richards said the following of his colleague *'There were plenty of people who wanted him dead and for very good reasons. Someday the truth will come out'* (Giuliano, vii, 1994).

On 15th September 2009 the Los Angeles Reuters ran a report by Dean Goodman, headlined *'New suspect emerges in possible Brian Jones murder'* Sam Cutler a former road manager of *The Rolling Stones* pointed the finger at the band's former chauffeur and security aid. Allegedly, Tom Keylock coaxed a death bed confession out of his friend Frank Thorogood. The latter had been staying in the flat at Cotchford Farm with his girlfriend and they were two of the last few people to have seen Jones alive on the 2nd July 1969 in the evening (www.reuters.com/article/us-jones).

There was no hard evidence linking either Keylock or Thorogood to the death of Jones in his swimming pool. However, Keylock had acted suspiciously in the ensuing days after his death removing and destroying items from Jones's home, which included valuable possessions such as a William Morris tapestry covered with fairies and elves (Hotchner, 1990, 313), other items included his bible, clothes, private papers and all of his guitars from the music studio (Giuliano, 1994, 161).

Cutler further disclosed that Keylock was the only suspect in a hitherto-undisclosed private investigation. This had been launched by *The Rolling Stones'* business adviser Allen Klein, who had little faith in the British police and used all the resources available to him to open the enquiry as he believed that Jones had been murdered.

He added in a blog post from www.gimmecutler.com that *'Tom Keylock was the prime (and only) suspect named in their report'*, he was never formally interviewed by the police (www.reuters.com). Ironically Keylock died on the same date as Jones on 2nd July although it was the year 2009 and Allen Klein died on 4th July in 2009.

On Saturday 5th July 1969 *The Rolling Stones* performed a free concert at Hyde Park in London which they dedicated to Jones. Ironically, a concert had already been scheduled to take place there so that the group could introduce their fans to the new member of the band Mick Taylor. Before the set began Mick Jagger read *Adonis,* a poem by Percy Byshe Shelley which was about the death of his poet friend John Keats. Stagehands released hundreds of white butterflies as part of the tribute to Jones.

Sam Cutler who was present at the concert recalled how *'The press was totally unsympathetic to Brian's demise, but the youth of his generation felt otherwise'* (Cooper & James, 2020, Cutler). He concluded that *'It was a moment thousands of people were not only mourning his passing but basically of the opinion that the poor guy had been virtually hounded to death'.*

On Thursday 10th July 1969, Jones was laid to rest in his home town of Cheltenham and thousands of people lined the streets to pay their respects to him. Charlie Watts and Bill Wyman were amongst the mourners. The service was held at the 900 year old parish church of Cheltenham and was led by Canon Hugh Evan Hopkin.

He read aloud with the permission of Mr and Mrs Jones, a telegram that their son sent to them when he came into conflict with the law which simply said *'Please don't judge me too harshly'.* The scripture reading was the story of the prodigal son (Giuliano, 1994, 182). Jones was buried and the words on his headstone read' *In affectionate remembrance of Brian Jones'* (Wohlin, 205, photo-plate).

Jazz musician and founder of the Brian Jones Appreciation Society Phil Kent, obsessed with Jones since 1963 said of him *'Brian was beautiful, sensitive, intelligent and exceptionally* talented ... A huge amount of abuse was pitted against him, but he was made an example of because he broke all the rules ... It is the memory that needs to be kept alive' (Giuliano, 1994, 197).

Creatives and musical artistes were devastated by the sudden death of the original founder and leader of *The Rolling Stones*. Some penned poems as an outpouring of their grief and dedication to the life of Brian Jones. For example, *The Who's* Pete Townshend wrote a poem called *A Normal Day for Brian, A Man Who Died Every Day* and it was published in *The Times* newspaper. Jim Morrison of *The Doors* wrote a poem entitled *ODE to LA While Thinking of Brian Jones Deceased* and Jimi Hendrix dedicated a song to his friend on US television.

In 1971 Reprise records released the album *Desertshore* by Nico, track one *Janitor of Lunacy* was composed as a tribute to Jones. Later in the mid nineteen eighties Temple Records released *Godstar* by Psychic TV which was written by Genesis P-Orridge and Alex Fergusson. In 1990 an American musical project and band led by Anton Newcombe called *The Brian Jonestown Massacre* was formed in San Francisco. The band's name is a portmanteau of both Jones's name and the 1978 cult leader Jim Jones self-dubbed *Jonestown* rural community in *Guyana*. There over 900 of his followers died in a mass murder suicide this became known as the Jonestown Massacre (en.wikipedia.org/wiki).

Ironically, Hendrix and Morrison both died within the following two years after Jones. All three men died aged twenty-seven. Today the trio are part of the mythology that is known as *The 27 Club,* This cultural phenomenon started between 1969–1971 with their deaths, along with Janis Joplin and Jim Morrison who all died aged twenty-seven. Interestingly, the American blues musician and songwriter

Robert Johnson (one of Jones's heroes) also died at the same age.

Sadly, and more recently the names of singers Kurt Cobain and Amy Winehouse have also been added to the *27 Club* for they also died at this age. The documentary and film industry has also paid homage to the life of Brian Jones. In 2005 the film *Stoned* was released. It was an account of Jones's role in *The Rolling Stones* and was directed by Stephen Woolley, the part of 'Brian' was played by English actor Leo Gregory. In 2019 the film *Rolling Stone, Life and Death of Brian Jones* was released, it was directed by Danny Garcia.

At the time of writing in 2023 the BBC's flagship Arts programme *Arena* released the documentary *The Stones and Brian Jones*, directed by and with Nick Broomfield who first met Jones on a train when they were both teenagers. Clearly, the love and curiosity about the life and death of Brian Jones has never faded away (pun intended!).

Mick Jagger said of Jones that he *'lived his life very fast … we took his one thing away which was his band'* (Broomfield, 2023, Magnolia Pictures). London journalist, Pete Cole said of Jones that he *'was made and destroyed by the times in which he lived'* (Aftel, 1982, 15). One of Jones's thousands of fans Paul Rayner, expressed his grief for him as well as acknowledging his genius musicianship and the difference in the *Rolling Stones* music, commenting *'… for me they were never the same after '69 when we lost Brian'* (Houghton, 2015, 205). Prince Stash clearly adored Jones and still does, declaring *'I miss him a great deal. I loved the guy'* (Houghton, 2015, 271).

'Brian Jones was a born nonconformist who couldn't accept any aspect of the world he was born into' (Hotchner, 1990, 374).

PART TWO

What Brian Jones's Natal Chart Reveals and the Astrology in Action

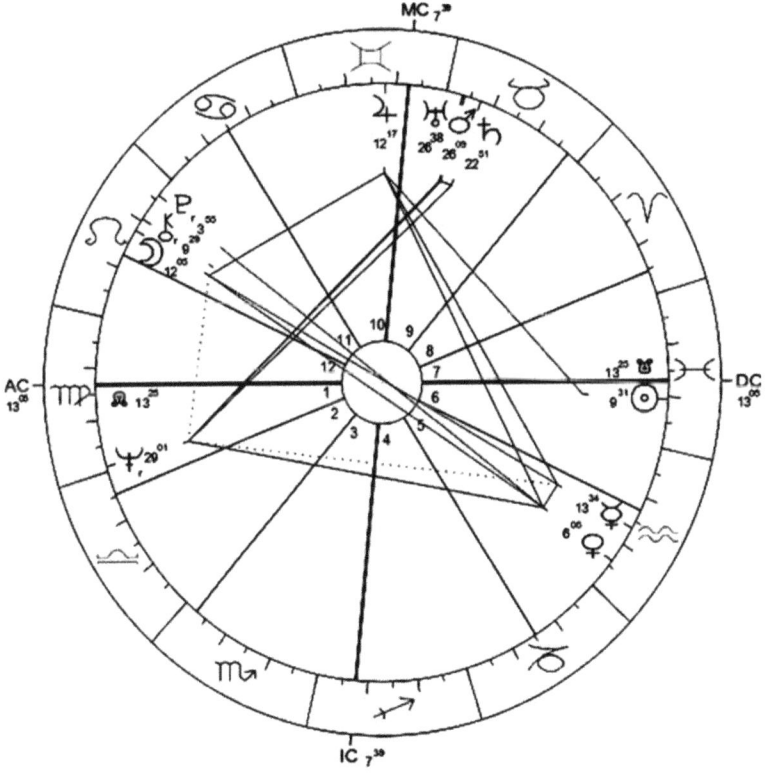

Brian Jones was named Lewis Brian Hopkin Jones and from here onwards he will primarily be referred to as 'Jones'. He was born on Saturday, 28th February 1942 in Cheltenham,

Gloucestershire. At the time of his birth which is believed to be 7pm (www.astro.com) the Sun was in Pisces and the Moon in Leo. This indicates that he was artistic, original and sensitive as well as having qualities for direction and leadership and an appreciation for drama and performance.

The Leo Moon was in the Gibbous Moon phase on his date of birth. Astrologer and author Raven Kaldera calls this phase of the lunation cycle the *'Singer's Moon'* which is most apt for Jones. He observed that people born under the *'Singer's Moon'* have a strong need for creative self-expression and that those born under a Leo Moon love to perform for their loved ones (Kaldera, 2011, 162).

Indeed, Jones invited his parents several times to come and watch him play with *The Rollin' Stones* but they never accepted his invitation, probably because they thought the group's music was abhorrent. It is well known that Mr and Mrs Jones did not approve of their son's decision to be in a band especially one that played rhythm and blues music.

However, some of his girlfriends, such as Linda Lawrence and Dawn Molloy were passionate about his music and were more than willing to be part of his audience, for they loved the genre of rhythm 'n' blues and of course Jones himself! It was not unusual for one of them to be backstage watching from the wings as Jones performed with his band to the pleasure of the hysterical screaming fans.

Jones vividly engaged with the audience as he performed on stage with the band, joking with and teasing his worshipping fans. Alan Miles recalls seeing *The Rollin' Stones* at Leyton Baths in 1963 and was in the crowd some three feet away from Jones. From there he had a good view of him playing his spearmint green Gretsch guitar (Houghton, 2015,

50). Miles recalled that many of the girls held up pictures of Jones. He remembered *'Brian studying one and his lips mockingly asked Who's That'*.

Another fan Viv Franklin remembered seeing *The Stones* and one thing that vividly stuck in his mind was that Mick Jagger told the audience that Brian Jones was delayed and might not make it to the gig, only for the crowd to see Jones peeping through the curtains at the back of the stage. At that point everyone went wild (Houghton, 2015, 47). Fan David Wheeler recounted that, when he was in the audience watching a *Stones* gig, Jones's guitar string broke and he proceeded to taunt the crowd with it before finally throwing it into the middle of the audience. Wheeler said he recalled how the floor was going up and down as the fans jumped up to try and catch the guitar string (Houghton, 2015, 95).

PISCES & NEPTUNE

Returning now to the astrology and Jones's Sun sign Pisces ...

The sign is ruled by Neptune and in mythology Neptune is God of the oceans and sea. The trident glyph for Neptune with its' three prongs symbolises the mind, body and spirit. This is a concept prevalent and established into our culture today, one obvious example being the Mind, Body and Spirit festivals. The symbol for Pisces is two fish swimming in opposite directions which are tied together. Given that fish do not swim in any specific way this suggests that Pisceans may have to make the choice as to whether they swim upstream or drift downstream metaphorically speaking.

In anatomy, and medical astrology, the following are associated with Pisces. The body part is the feet, the area which enables us to connect to the Earth's ley lines and their subtle energies. In this sense it could be said that our feet bond us with spiritual dimensions. The pineal gland, and those parts of the nervous system which are receptive to psychic impressions along with the chakras and human aura, are also associated with this sign.

Pisces is one of the three water signs (the other two being Cancer and Scorpio) and suggests that Jones had a strongly developed intuition, a vivid imagination as well as psychic and mediumistic abilities. Interestingly, water is pertinent to what we know of Jones's history in that he was a strong swimmer, he also crossed the seas in his many long-distance travels, and tragically he drowned in his swimming pool at Cotchford Farm.

Astrologically, Neptune is associated with many different areas and themes such as: art, ballet and dance, fashion, dreams, glamour, the film industry, illusion, magic, healing, music, imagination, spirituality, transcendence, poetry, writing and photography. Regarding transcendence, Jones had an interest in Transcendental Meditation (TM) which was developed by Maharishi Mahesh Yogi.

He went to Bremen, Germany to hear the Yogi lecture and he also got the opportunity to meet him (www.youtube.com). Apparently, when Jones spoke to him, he asked him if TM would help to remove what he named *'the horrors'*, which were unreasonable fears that Jones was prone to (Prince Stash in conversation with author). What the Yogi's reply was we do not know, but it does show that by Jones asking the question that he was capable of self-reflection in realising that his trepidations of *'the horrors'* were irrational.

Other correspondences of Neptune include: mystics and psychics as well as places of confinement such as hospitals and prisons, other connections include alcohol, drugs, medicine and illness. All of these things touched Jones's life. Further subjects associated with Neptune include addiction, being without boundaries, confusion, deception, escape, disillusion, infiltration, loss, sacrifice, the underdog and victimisation. Qualities such as: compassion, empathy, forgiveness, sensitivity and vulnerability are also associated with Neptune as well as being idealistic and commitment-shy.

Jones was interviewed in 1965 on the film *Rolling Stones: Charlie Is My Darling* and was questioned about marriage, Jones revealed that *'The whole prospect of, marriage rather frightens me. It's rather like signing a contract ... If I could get married for a year and just sign a year's contract I'd probably be much happier at the thought of getting married'* (Whitehead, ABCKO Films, Loog Oldham). As we can see there are vast numbers of correspondences associated with Pisces and its' ruler Neptune and so many of them are linked with Jones in his short lifetime.

Interestingly, some of Jones's colleagues, friends and girlfriends were also born under the sign of Pisces for example: Tara Browne the son of a peer and heir to a Guiness fortune. He was an Irish London based socialite and co-founder of *Dandie Fashions* in the Kings Road, Chelsea which was founded in 1966. He inspired John Lennon and Paul McCartney to re-write some of the verses in the song '*A Day In The Life Of*' after he was killed in a car accident in 1967. Tara Browne's wife Nicki said of her husband and Jones that *'their birthdays were within three or four days of each other.*

They were both Pisces. Free-spirited. Very moral in their ways, without ever being sanctimonious. They were like brothers to each other' (Howard, 2017, 200).

When Jones was door stepped by a reporter who broke the news of Browne's death to him he apparently wept uncontrollably and sobbed *'I am numbed … It's ghastly. He was so full of life'* (Howard, 2017, 293). That evening he went to visit Browne's widow *'He sat down and, without uttering a single word, she said, he played soothing guitar to her for two hours until she fell asleep'* (Howard, 217, 293).

Anita Pallenberg was also a close friend of Tara and said *'Brian was very sensitive and I think he recognised that Tara was sensitive too'* (Howard, 2017, 286). Nicki Browne also said of Tara *'Forever young. But he knew his time wasn't going to be long. He often said it'* (Howard, 2017, 306).

One thing that can be said of Tara Browne and Brian Jones is that they did have a genuine friendship together and it must have really torn Brian when his friend was killed. The grief must have been monumental. Pallenberg claimed that in the early months of 1966 *'Tara was about as close to Brian as anyone was allowed to get'* (Howard, 2017, 238). They would smoke pot, listen to *The Lovin Spoonful* and talk about life. Or they'd stay up all night at Eaton Row (Browne's home) drinking brandy and playing with Tara's Scalextric cars on the carpet.

Some of the other Piscean associations and relationships that Jones had were with George Harrison, Giorgio Gomelsky, Paul Jones and Dawn Molloy. George Harrison's album *Brainwashed* was released posthumously in 2002. Harrison outlived Jones by thirty-two years and died of cancer in 2001.

Brainwashed was Harrison's final studio album; he wrote a hymn like song for it called *Pisces Fish*.

It was an autobiographical song where symbolism and themes of Pisces are evident throughout. For example, lyrics such as, '… I'm a Pisces fish and the river runs through my soul … I think of all the Gods and what they feel. You can only find them in the deepest silence' (www.beatlesbible.com).

Harrison reflected affectionately on Jones after he died '*I got to know him very well and I felt very close to him … I often met him in times of trouble … I don't think he had enough love and understanding. He was very nice, sincere and sensitive, and we must remember that's who he was*' (Giuliano, 1994, 194).

Giorgio Gomelsky said of himself and Brian '*I kind of let myself be a friend of his because we were both born on the 28th February. You can't go wrong, born on the same day. It's not the same year, but the same day. Pisces lunatics. Big mistake …*' (Dumaurier, 2023, 43). Gomelsky also warned Jones somewhat prophetically in the earlier years when the band was still in its' infancy '*I warned him. I told him, I have no doubt that you'll get there, but be careful when you get there.*

Dawn Molloy recalled that Jones used to have prescient and vivid dreams and that he also had a belief in the afterlife (Dawn Molloy in correspondence to author). This shows that as a young man Jones was already spiritually evolving, perhaps he had already started way before he met Dawn Molloy.

Linda Lawrence has astrological knowledge and observed that Jones '*was very money-conscious, but Pisces seem to be*' (Balfour, 1986, 81). He certainly knew what it was like to experience food and financial poverty. He recalled how before the band was successful, how *'There was a time when all I lived on was an egg beaten up in mashed potato'* (Giuliano, 1994, 243). In 1966 he commented in interview that *'We had enough hard times, with people laughing up their sleeves at us and we were the ones who had to show real determination'* (Dalton, 1980, 28).

Addressing the issue of earnings and finances he said *'We know that money is important. But we're in this business principally because we enjoy it, because we get pleasure out of it. Cut off the money and you'll still find us playing this kind of music ... even if we have to go back to bumming drinks off people to keep going'.*

Lawrence also declared *'My relationship with Brian was so Karmic* (sic), *so very different from any others that met him.* (Cooper & James, 2020, Lawrence, Ireland 2019). She along with Dawn Molloy, also knew that he was very spiritual and believed in dreams (correspondence to author). Both women must have had many an interesting conversation with Jones about his beliefs and dreams.

On the night of the 2nd July 1969, Dawn Molloy was awoken by a menacing and vivid dream. Eerily, she had a prophetic vision that Jones had drowned in a swimming pool (Young, 2013, 199). She remembered the detail of the dream which included that he *'... saw me and reached his hand out to mine. His hair was floating out around him and he had a terrified look in his eyes'*. Clearly, his distressed spirit was reaching out for help and his communication was received by Dawn in her sleep-state. It must have been an alarming and unnerving time for her when she learnt through the media on the 3rd July that Jones had drowned the night before.

Keith Richards commented on the *'constantly shifting triangle'* between himself, Jagger and Jones *'There was something between us that didn't quite make it somewhere. Maybe it's in the stars. He was a Pisces, I'm a Sagittarius and Mick's a Leo. Maybe those three can't ever completely connect all together at the same time for very long'* (Guiliano, 1994, 25). Richards was correct to a degree in his thinking. This is because the strong mutable (*see glossary*) energy in Jones's natal chart is uncomfortable with permanence. Maybe it was simply a case with those three individuals that 'two's company three's a crowd'.

ORIGINAL THINKING, RELATIONSHIPS & SEXUALITY

In Jones's natal chart the descendant (*see glossary*) is in Pisces and this angle is directly opposite the ascendant (*see glossary*). It corresponds to relationships in terms of what one is attracted to, what one draws towards them as well as what one needs from a partner. The Pisces qualities (as already observed) include areas such as being: artistic, compassionate, dreamy, glamorous, musically able, romantic and sensitive.

One illustration of Jones's romantic nature can be seen in his writing of letters, postcards and occasional poetry to his girlfriends, one example being a poem to Linda Lawrence called *Thank You For Being There My Love'*. The message of the prose expresses his thanks to her for being in his life at the time that she was, and for finding in her qualities of authenticity and sincerity which were vital to him at that period of his life (Cooper & James, 2020, Lawrence, Ireland 2019). Jones's sensitivity wasn't exclusive only to this area of writing. He was finely tuned into areas of delicacy such as; atmospheres, undercurrents, auras and psychic realms as we shall learn later through various examples.

Mercury and Venus are in the fifth house of his natal chart the area associated with recreation, children and romantic relationships. It suggests that Jones looked for a partner who was as intelligent and witty as himself, and who was mentally stimulating and enjoyed learning new things as he did. Marianne Faithfull described how when she first found herself caught up with *The Rolling Stones* that she didn't know much about music at that stage. She told author A. E. Hotchner that Jones *'who was very knowledgeable, got me interested in it. He could talk about anything. He was a very eclectic person'* (Giuliano, 1994, 185) which shows what a great conversationalist he could be as well as inspiring.

Jones's friend Prince Stash saw a better change in his friend when he first got together with Anita Pallenberg remarking how much happier Jones had seemed in years. He described how *'She demanded intellectual stimulation … He was a very gentle person who enjoyed conversation and his mind was avid for an esoteric kind of love'* (Howard, 2017, 216). Marianne Faithfull remembered many a conversation with Jones and wrote that *'He was so intelligent and would become very animated when the subject interested him. Trains, Ingmar Bergman movies, anything magical'* (Faithfull, 1995, 87).

He certainly loved to love, however the demonstration and meaning of love came with it's challenges to Jones and impacted significantly on some of his partners. Mercury's restless energy and need for variety manifested itself in

Jones's life by him having an active romantic life. Mars in Taurus suggests that as a lover he may have been affectionate and could master the art of seduction, with a great appetite for sex and the stamina to go with it. The empathic and sensitive side of his Piscean nature may well have added to knowing what a partner wanted when making love which would have enhanced his technique and potentially made him selfless in this area. Certainly, this seems to have been the case in his earlier lifetime. His live-in girlfriend at Cotchford Farm, Anna Wohlin, *'soon realised that Brian craved affection and that he needed to know that he was desirable and loved'* (Wohlin, 2005, 55).

Dawn Molloy became Jones's girlfriend when she was eighteen years old. She vividly commented on his sexual prowess in the recent BBC Arena documentary *'The Stones and Brian Jones'*. She said of him he was *'very sexy – the way he made love he was just insatiable – an amazing teacher of how you should make love to a woman'* (Broomfield, 2023, Magnolia Pictures).

Jeremy Reed author of *'Brian Jones The Last Decadent'*, said of Jones that he was the *'intransigent, bisexual zeitgeist of a generation beginning to scent its' explosive potential'* (Reed, 1999, 38). He further added that Jones's *'contributions to gay culture were suppressed by a management intent on marketing the Rolling Stones as a product of subversive machismo'*. With the exception of Nicholas Fitzgerald biographers have made little issue of Jones's sexual relations with men.

He added *'I would go so far as to say that it was the gay components of Brian's complex gender orientation which accounted for his creative panache as a musician, and as a fashion leader to his generation'*. Reed's perceptions hold credibility given the discussion that Jones had with his close friend Nicholas Fitzgerald.

The latter commented in his autobiography (*Brian Jones: The Inside Story of The Original Rolling Stone*) that he and Jones entered into a long conversation '*over Brian's belief that most people are bisexual*' and added that '*They're just too uptight to admit it or practice it ... A lot of people in rock are ambidextrous as far as sex is concerned*' (Fitzgerald, 1985, 89). The definition of the word bisexual has evolved throughout the years as well as terms regarding gender and sexuality (www.stonewall.org.uk/about-us/news/short-history-word-bisexuality).

Returning now to the astrology in Jones's natal chart and looking at his communication and mentality which we can see through Mercury in Aquarius. It shows that he was mentally bright, progressive and original; an intelligent rebel. Positioned in the fifth house Mercury suggests he was an inventor and was able to pick up new ideas out of the air. This is emphatically borne out by him being self-taught on almost any instrument, a genius and natural musician for sure.

Mercury in Aquarius also indicates that Jones could arrive at his own ideas and formulate his opinions independently. He was interested in truths as he saw them and as such could be knowledgeable and open-minded. This theme is also seen by the position of Jupiter in Gemini in his natal chart. Anita Pallenberg said of Jones '*He wanted to know everything ... which is why he wanted to meet people who were different from him*'. *He was always investigating the truth about things*' (Howard, 217, 199). By being open-minded, social and versatile this was a way that opportunities could present themselves to Jones. He discussed his controversial ideas openly and was not afraid of contradicting others.

When interviewed on radical subjects, areas that Jones spoke about included the (then) controversial topics of unmarried couples living together, as well as signing a yearly contract for marriage. There was also the subject of his Rolls-Royce Silver Cloud which had a car registration number plate of DD-666 (Devil's Disciple 666). The number 666 being attributed to the anti-Christ or the Great Beast which no doubt will have offended some religious groups. Jones commented that *'In another age they would have burned me'* recognising how the number plate would have outraged and roused certain people. The *Great Beast* was also the name attributed to the notorious occultist Aleister Crowley. (Giulian, 1994, 55).

Venus in Aquarius suggests that Jones enjoyed unconventional relationships with forward thinking partners and where individuality could thrive. There may not have been a huge dividing line between his friends and lovers, for example where the friends easily become the lovers. In addition, they may have come from all different backgrounds as Jones would be open to mixing with persons irrespective of their class, income, colour or creed. For him it was individuality, perhaps somebody outside of their own predictable circle and free-spirited individuals (especially women) whom he would have been attracted to and, equally, where people were attracted to him. Freedom, space and tolerance are areas associated with Venus in Aquarius and would have been alluring to him in all relationships.

This message is further emphasised by the aspect of Venus trine Uranus (the latter the ruler of Aquarius) where differences, freedom and originality were valuable to Jones, especially if excitement, detachment and experimentalism were part of his relationships. He would not have been offended by what some others may have viewed as unconventional relationships, such as open relationships and same-sex relationships.

Being conventional and predictable would not have appealed to Jones. One example of this is borne out by the following. His good friend Ronni Money spoke of how when he was in a relationship with Pallenberg that she '*was into the bisexual number and arranged scenes*' (Reed, 1998, 74) for her and Brian.

Disconnection, objectivity and separation are areas connected with Aquarius and it's ruler Uranus. Therefore, the position of Venus in Aquarius suggests that for him being able to relate to others where there was no emotional involvement and permanence would have been more fulfilling, although not necessarily satisfying to his partner(s). Jeremy Reed summed up Jones's remote and indifferent nature as '*dissociation from commitment, and a cold sense of detachment from emotional involvement*' (Reed, 1999, 59).

The impersonal nature theme is also echoed by the Moon in eleventh house where it indicates an instinctive need for experimentation and freedom. Reed also commented '*Any study of Brian Jones will point to the essential isolation he felt as an individual. One suspects that he lacked the ability to be close with anyone*' (Reed, 1999, 70) which speaks of some of the message behind Venus in Aquarius.

Jones's friend Ronni Money recalled how, one evening, he wanted somebody to stay with him and that he was prepared to pay for their company, not for sex but for companionship.

He asked Money if she would be able to find a woman for him. Jones admitted that he knew the potential person would be with him for the money and not just because he was a member of *The Stones*, he said *'I don't know whether people want to be with me because I'm me or cos I'm Brian Jones of the Rolling Stones'* (Aftel, 1982, 139/140). Company was found for him that evening and the woman said afterwards of Jones that *'He was so nice. All he wanted to do was talk and I cuddled him a little'* (Aftel, 1982, 140).

Author Gary Herman commented that Jones's *'total insecurity was reflected in the reputation he had acquired for near satyriasis'* (Herman, 44, 1982). This is the term given to males who have an abnormal or excessive sexual desire which is disruptive to life or overall health (www.collinsdictionary.com). Herman continued that *'60 women a month was the figure bandied about'* (Herman, 44, 1982) regarding Jones and his conquests.

Eric Burdon singer in *The Animals* spent time unwinding with Jones in some of the London clubs after his band and *The Stones* were on tour together. He said of him *'I knew him and yet I didn't know him'* (Trynka, 2014, 117) continuing *'He seemed to be obsessed with hookers, which was strange'*.

He also recognised the independent and innovative drive in Jones compared to the other members of *'The Stones'*. He said of him that he was *'The one wanting to stretch out and be inventive'*. This latter comment illustrates the original and progressive thinking of the Mercury in Aquarius position.

Jones was interviewed when *The Stones* were touring in Austria and was asked about the (then) released album *'Their Satanic Majesties Request'* which was very different to the band's previous commercial style. He replied *'I think *everybody should experiment ... we don't want to continue along a tangential line. Every now and then we want to go out and experiment'* (Giulliano, 1994, 245). Years later Keith Richards confessed that *'Brian was always the first to bring in other people's culture and music to the band* (Jackson, 1992, 170).

Jones's enthusiasm for other societies and faraway places can be seen in a letter he wrote in 1967 to his friend art dealer and gallery owner Robert Fraser (also known as 'Groovy Bob'). The latter was imprisoned for being in possession of heroin and was sentenced to six months hard labour at HM Wormwood Scrubs Prison (www.en.wikipedia.org/wiki/Robert_Fraser).

Jones was excited about going to visit Libya and told Fraser *'I'm planning to leave on Friday for Tripoli then dig some oases in the Libyan desert ... I hope to find a groovy scene there.* The letter also included Jones's apology for not having written sooner but he *'spent a month doing a nursing home scene then I spent a freaky month in Spain'* (Wyner, 1999, 211).

CHARM, PRESENCE & STYLE

The Venus and Uranus aspect also indicates that Jones could fall in and out of love very suddenly and that his relationships might be erratic. They may also have been electrically exciting; this is due to the shocking, and unpredictable, nature of Uranus.

Astrologer, and author, Sue Tomkins observed that people with this aspect in their natal chart are also likely to have a marked feature of originality in artistic and creative fields, and that the person would likely to deviate from the classic styles to be expected of them from their background, training or upbringing (Tomkins, 1989, 191). This is borne out by the genius musicianship that Jones brought to the music of the band that he formed, as well as his bohemian and distinctive stylishness that was markedly his.

Dawn Molloy recalled that in the earlier *Stones* years when she went to see them play at one particular gig that as she and her friend were leaving early in order to beat the crowds there was the ringing in their ears of the band playing *Route 66*. She was left with a vivid impression of Jones *'What I had noticed was an immaculately dressed blond haired angel, wearing very fine striped trousers with matching waistcoat, white shirt and string tie'* (Young, 2013, 65). Clearly, he left a distinct and marked effect on her that evening.

Aside from relationships Venus is also associated with beauty, charm, grace, panache and style which Jones oozed plenty of. This is a pointer in his natal chart via the aspect of Venus trine Jupiter. He was described by Dawn Molloy as having *'high powered charm'* (Young, 2013, 83) and that *'His manners were impeccable'* (Young, 2013, 69).

His slight lisp she found endearing (Young, 2013, 83) she commented *'His voice was soft, with well-spoken Queen's English'* (Young, 2013, 68). She also remembered that when she was in a physical relationship with Jones that he used to wear Cedar Wood cologne (Young, 2013, 105) and at times, when she was close to him, she could smell the fragrance of Imperial soap on him (popular cosmetics of the time) (Young, 2013, 74). Marianne Faithfull also commented on his manners in her autobiography *Faithfull*, stating that *'Brian had lovely manners and a little whispery voice'* (Faithfull, 1995, 87).

Many people commented on his long hair which was considered outrageous in the nineteen sixties especially by the older generation, although younger fans loved it. Fan Sonny Thrower recalled how Jones's *'hair and style really made him stand out in spite of Mick's dancing … Brian exuded such elegant class and grace, he was clearly the Stones creator and different from the rest'* (Houghton, 2015, 245).

Eric Burdon had great respect for Jones and acknowledged his presence on stage, commenting that Jagger and Richards were *'in the shadows, Because on the side is this blond-haired Aryan dude on guitar, and you couldn't help but look at him. He had this magnetism about him, you couldn't escape it. But it was twisted'* (Trynker, 2014, 117).

Other fans were equally impressed by his hair and general demeanour. Ken Magill saw *The Rollin Stones* in concert and recalled *'I was transfixed by the length of Brian Jones's hair. He had the longest hair of all the guys by quite some bit'* (Houghton, 2015, 52) and Christine Murphy recalled how *'Brian was cool, his long blond hair moving as he played'* (Houghton, 2015, 53).

In 1967 London ballet student Natasha Conn was seated in a coffee shop in the Kings' Road. She turned around and saw Jones speaking with Russian dancer Rudolf Nureyev the former was wearing *'a purple jacket, with white cuffs practically flowing to the floor'* (Houghton, 2015, 270). Biographer Paul Trynka regarded Jones as a pioneer and described him as *'an aesthetic revolutionary, a peacock, a Regency dandy re-envisioned for a psychedelic era'* (Cooper & James, 2020, an appreciation Paul Trynka).

Prince Stash recalled how he and Jones had the utmost disdain *'for the straight world, for the bowler hat brigade for the drabness of western menswear'* as well as *'necessity to avoid the cheap boutique alternatives of 'groovy gear' offered to all and sundry by Carnaby Street'* (Cooper & James, 2020, Clothes or the Peacock Imperative). Instead, they went shopping in antiquarian markets which sold used women's clothes, this activity they referred to as *'scoring chick's clothes'*. They sought to find *'dazzling embroidered Oriental garb, plumed hats, lace ruffles, silk, satin, velvet trousers, buckle shoes'*

As well as these items they also looked for silk mini dresses that could be turned into tunics, elaborate Arab caftans, flamenco dancer shirts and satin capes. His revolutionary capacity is also seen by the following comment of New York journalist Al Aronowitz who said, *'Jones was the first man I ever knew to wear costume jewellery bought in the lady's department at Saks'* (Giuliano, 1994, 47). Saks being an American luxury department store chain.

Both Jones and Pallenberg created a revolutionary androgynous style; they mixed and matched fabrics and patterns as well as centuries and cultures. Jones thought nothing of exhibiting himself through the streets of London wearing items such as a Victorian lace shirt, floppy turn of the century hat, Edwardian velvet frock coat, multi-coloured suede boots, along with scarves hanging from his neck, waist and legs as well as Berber antique jewellery (Giuliano, 1994, 47). Given that cross-dressing in the mid to late nineteen sixties was largely exercised in discreet places or behind closed doors, the androgyny that Jones and Pallenberg were parading was more than radical for that period of time. When Jones started to dress as a symbol of androgyny swathed in silks and velvets (Cooper & James, 2020, heading *He was the most gifted* …) Caroline Coon perceived that *'His appearance was a political statement – because he was blurring gender with* long hair, flowing clothes, his love of external cultures. And for that he was vulnerable'.

ABUSE, CONTROL & DESTRUCTION

The Venus opposing Pluto aspect in Jones's natal chart suggests that at times he could have been intensely emotional which may have created problems in his relationships. Areas such as jealousy, paranoia and resentment are some of the less helpful characteristics associated with Pluto. Potentially Jones may have alienated those that he was closest to by demonstrating such excessive qualities. Examples of his paranoia, jealousy and possessiveness have frequently been commented upon. Pallenberg recalled how they *'had a massive row everywhere we went. Caused by jealousy, possessiveness from his side, insecurity from his side. I was far more mellow'* (Howard, 2017, 240).

She elaborated that Jones *'used to throw me out. He used to get so violent and then he just put me outside the door and I didn't know where to go and I used to run over to Nicki and Tara to lick my wounds. I spent many nights there. Then the next morning I would go back home* (Howard, 2017, 240). Whilst loving his freedom in a relationship it may have been a case of *'do as I say and not as I do'*. If this was true it shows that Jones had double-standards in this area of his life.

Pat Andrews was also subjected to his jealousy. They became a couple but he felt threatened by her male friends. On one occasion he found a letter from one of Andrews' old boyfriends. He ripped it up in front of all their friends in one of their frequented coffee bars. *'He wanted Pat's complete attention and his freedom at the same time'*. Everyone who knew the couple knew that Andrews was absolutely devoted to Jones (Aftel, 1982, 28). The couple argued frequently and one night whilst they were fighting *'Brian blackened Pat's eye and she ran home'* (Aftel, 1982, 33).

Returning to the astrology again ...

The Pisces descendant in his natal chart suggests a desire to merge with one's partner on a soul level and to find a fulfilling spiritual connection. The Sun is near to the descendant and indicates that Jones could attract partners who wanted to be the centre of his world perhaps even stealing his distinctive spotlight if he let them. One obvious example of the latter is with the independent Pallenberg who was a successful actress; model, artist, and multi-linguist.

Her natal chart indicates that she could be assertive and forceful therefore potentially taking Jones's individuality from him. He told Anna Wohlin that *'he had been completely controlled by Anita and although he realised that their relationship had been destructive and doomed to failure, he couldn't leave her'* (Wohlin, 2005, 131). Wohlin concluded however, *'I'm convinced though, that they were both to blame for their confused relationship'*.

The absorbing energy of Pisces coupled with Neptune in the first house of his natal chart would have made this merge virtually effortless. Jones's friend, Ronni Money recalled a conversation between her and Jones where he claimed that *'... Anita was like a sponge that drained everything out of him. She didn't allow him any time to rest; she was all me, me, me'* (Giuliano, 1994, 57). Clearly, Money had concerns for her friend.

Interestingly, Pallenberg also has the Sun positioned in the sixth house of her natal chart (see part 3/Fig.4) although it is not as near to the descendant as Jones's. Friends of the couple saw how they were merging together in physical terms as well as in personality. In terms of their appearance, they have been described as *'the first truly interchangeable couple'* and were ahead of merging couples such as John and Yoko and David and Angie Bowie (Wells, 2021, 59).

Friend Terry Southern remembered that *'the thing that caused the sophistos at Annabel's and Scott's Piccadilly* (clubs) *to gawk like bumpkins-was not just the bewitching beauty of the couple, but the startling resemblance to each other'*. Marianne Faithfull remembered affectionately how *'They were the spitting image of each other and not an ounce of modesty existed between them'* she continued *'I would sit mesmerised for hours, watching them preening in the mirror, trying on each other's clothes. All roles and gender would evaporate in these narcissistic performances'*. In terms of personality unification their behaviour was not as endearing, instead it was cruel and spiteful towards some others as seen by the following examples.

Linda Lawrence and son Julian still an infant, went to see Jones at his home that he shared with Pallenberg in Courtfield Road. The reason for the visit was that Lawrence said that she had been distressed by the lack of support from Jones both financially and otherwise for their son.

Consequently, Mr Lawrence, his daughter and grandson travelled to Kensington to confront Jones (Wells, 2021, 70). However, Lawrence was humiliated for she received no response after ringing the doorbell, *'they put on an emotional display at street level, at one point holding up Brian's baby'*.

Jones and Pallenberg looked out of their bay window from their upstairs flat and refused to invite the mother and son into their home. Instead, they just looked at Lawrence and Julian who remained outside on the pavement whilst the couple apparently *'cackled at the sight of the distraught pair gesticulating in the street'*.

Lawrence described how she *'felt devastated'* and that it was horrible. She described to interviewer Nick Broomfield that when Jones started to hang out with Anita that it was her influence that brought out his dark side. She added that the dynamic in Lawrence and Jones's relationship was never dark, unlike his and Pallenberg's (Broomfield, 2023, Magnolia Pictures). Another example, of their sinister influence with each other is when they used to 'spike' other people's drinks with either alcohol or drugs.

The Sun close to the descendant in Jones's natal chart also suggests that he needed a companion to make him feel complete but where he could still be his own unique person and remain true to himself. In having a partner it could either help or hinder development to his personality, when he needed to find an even greater confidence to express his own identity fully.

In 1969 and well after his relationship had dissolved with Pallenberg, he revealed to Anna Wohlin that their (Jones and Pallenberg) *'life together was a constant see-saw between drugs and fights … We were always competing with each other for the most attention … just getting the attention was the main thing'* (Wohlin, 2005, 132).

Seemingly, he was rarely without a romantic partner however long or short lived the relationship was. Less positive energies of the Piscean descendant can include addiction, escapism, irresponsible partners, deceit and pretence. Jones also told Wohlin that he '*was relieved not to have ended up addicted to heroin like Anita, Keith and Marianne Faithfull*' (Wohlin, 2005, 132).

He continued and reflected '*But I realise now that drugs are an escape and I don't want to run the risk of ending up like I was before, or like some of my former friends. That's why I try not to give in when I long for something.* Pallenberg recalled that when Jones first took acid at their mutual friend Robert Fraser's house. (Hotchner, 1990, 192) that he saw creatures coming out of the floors, ground and walls and he searched the cupboards looking for people (Giuliano, 1994, 47).

The Virgo ascendant is directly opposite the Piscean descendant. One interpretation of this rising sign is that Jones may have wanted to analyse and organise his partner's life. He may also have been agitated and restless at times which may have made him prickly. Another interpretation of this position is that he may have liked to busy himself in his partner's life and at other times could be forceful too. One small illustration of this is borne out in Jones's personal life by him organising his girlfriend Linda Lawrence to attend modelling school in London. She was already attending a hairdressing school and became a talented hairstylist (Broomfield, 2023, Magnolia Pictures). Indeed, it was her who created Jones's distinctive and original hairstyle and encouraged him to keep it long, and only ever trimmed it for him so that it kept its' length. As previously said men with long hair in the nineteen sixties were considered scandalous and by Lawrence creating such a hair style for Jones shows her own bohemian nature.

She described Jones at this point of her life as being *'so sensitive and he really knew who I was and how I was looking for my way'* (Cooper & James, 2020, Lawrence, Ireland 2019). Jones persuaded Lawrence to become a fashion model, as he thought there would be an opportunity for her to meet a variety of people, and he was correct in his thinking. Lawrence told author Mandy Aftel *'Brian brought me to a London modelling (sic) school because he thought I would meet different kinds of people'* (Aftel, 1983, 56), he also took her to all her modelling classes.

However, she said of the modelling industry that it *'was such a pushy thing. You had to do things you really didn't agree with'*. In 2019 she revealed that *'Brian saw my talents and made sure I met the important people in art, music, film and fashion, and through them I met others who became my lifelong teachers'* (Cooper & James, 2020, Lawrence, Ireland 2019). However, as previously observed we know that he also had an aggressive, controlling and jealous side to his nature as Lawrence and others experienced.

ADMINISTRATION, PERFECTION & TECHNIQUE

Neptune is in the first house of Jones's natal chart and in the final degree of Virgo. This is a critical degree as it indicates that he had a kind of mastery of experience in the areas associated with Virgo. Illustrations of this include: craft, intelligence, skill, analytical, hardworking, a purist and perfectionist as well as being familiar with anxiety, worry and physical health issues. Neptune rules chemicals and drugs whilst Virgo is concerned with maintenance of the body.

Certainly, we can see the Virgo ascendant in action by way of Jones's fastidious craftsmanship, skill and technique on his slide-guitar playing. Also, on the more exotic instruments that he played which all added to the distinct and recognisable sound of *The Stones* music, e.g. the slide guitar on *Little Red Rooster* and the flute on *Ruby Tuesday*.

The ascendant is also evident in the many health issues that Jones lived with. Virgo is also humble, modest and discerning, Jones often came across as such in many interviews thus illustrating the Virgo persona. Administration is also connected with this sign and certainly Jones was active in this way during the early days of the then *Rollin' Stones*. He undertook tasks such as arranging gigs by letter, telephoning potential hosts, as well as replying to fan-mail and organising payment for other band members.

One example of Jones's letter writing can be seen at the beginning of 1962 when he wrote to the BBC's *Jazz Club* on behalf of the band. He asked for *'The Rollin' Stones'* to be auditioned. He explained that *'Our musical policy is simply to produce an authentic Chicago Rhythm and Blues sound, using material of such R & B' greats as Muddy Waters, Howlin' Wolf, Bo Diddley, Jimmy Reed, and many others'* (Wyman & Havers, 2002, 44).

His pedantic nature is also illustrated whereby he wrote again to the *Jazz Club* in 1962 clarifying what form of music the term *Rhythm & Blues* should be applied to. He was emphatic that it most definitely could not be considered as a form of Jazz (Wyman & Havers, 2002, 39). Anna Wohlin observed the stickler side of his nature *'Brian was a perfectionist. He was never satisfied until he'd discovered the perfect sound. And when he found it he was so happy as could be and rang his friends to share his success'* (Wohlin, 2005, 105). She observed that he was also a perfectionist when it came to his food, and how it was cooked (Wohlin, 2005, 79).

The position of Neptune in the first house also suggests that Jones was attracted to fantasy, glamour and illusion. To some he may have appeared bewitching, ethereal and even spellbinding such are some of the qualities associated with Neptune. Interestingly, actress, model and singer Marilyn Monroe also had Neptune in the first house of her natal chart (www.astro.com/). She died of a drug overdose on the 5th August 1962.

PSYCHIC ABILITY, MEDIUMSHIP & SPIRIT ACTIVITY

The sensitive nature associated with Neptune and Pisces suggests that Jones was intuitive, mediumistic, psychic and easily able to tune-in to the vibrations around him and was at ease with these areas. Commentators, authors and researchers found this to be true and the subject is illustrated here by the following examples which show his psychic awareness and sensitivity.

Firstly, Jones was experienced and unperturbed by psychic phenomena and spirit activity something which was a frequent occurrence in some of his homes. For example, he told his friend Nicholas Fitzgerald that he had a ghost in the cottage at Cotchford Farm. He said *'It opens and closes doors, calls my name in a female voice'* (Fitzgerald, 1985, 45). He continued ... *'I have read a lot about the supernatural. It's a very deep subject. There are certain people who attract spirits.*

They have some kind of warmth about them that's felt by spirits'. When Fitzgerald asked Jones if he thought he attracted spirits he replied *'I don't know. I must if I have a ghost here, I suppose. I've never seen it but I do hear it'* (Fitzgerald, 1985, 46).

American fan Sonny Thrower also got to see the *Stones* in 1965 at the Civic Coliseum in Knoxville, Tennessee. He said *... getting to see Brian was miraculous. His stage presence was almost spiritual and it took some doing to get the live focus off of him ... Brian had a glow around him somehow and his spirit and passion were undeniable in that live stage performance'* (Houghton, 2015, 245). This shows how spiritually knowledgeable Thrower was in recognising the psychic and unworldly aura that surrounded Jones. It is also in keeping with what the latter explained to his friend Fitzgerald about certain people having warmth that attracts spirit and demonstrates his Piscean nature in terms of being interested in the mystical areas of life.

Richard Cadbury a friend of Fitzgerald and acquaintance of Jones, upon his first visit to Cotchford Farm told the former that the place was *'Impressive but creepy. Eerie'* (Fitzgerald 1985, 238). He continued *'I've got a weird sort of intuition, or imagination if you like. All houses have atmospheres, vibrations. Well, to me they do. And the vibes there were creepy'*. Fitzgerald laughed at his friend.

Anna Wohlin, the live-in girlfriend of Jones's at Cotchford Farm until he died wrote in her autobiography that he said *'There's a special magic in the house'* (Wohlin, 2005, 174). She also revealed that Jones was a firm believer in the after-life (Wohlin, 2005, 102) and used to enjoy telling stories about *'good natured – ghosts who walked the earth after their death'*. She continued that Jones told her a story about a young maid called Mary who in the past had worked in the house there and was buried in the garden, although the exact location of where she was buried was unknown to him. He also told his girlfriend that *'Mary had been a restless soul and that he tried to help her find peace'* (Wohlin, 205, 101).

This he did by inviting a few of his friends to Cotchford Farm amongst them Marianne Faithfull and John Lennon. Hashish *'billowed like a mist in the house as they played the music from Jajouka and said prayers for her. The party had been going on for several days and Brian said that he'd neither seen her nor heard her since then'*. Thus implying that their ritual intention to put Mary's soul to rest was fruitful, through using music and prayer.

Before Jones moved to Cotchford Farm, he already had experience of living with 'spirit activity' in his home. Colleague Bill Wyman wrote that during the spring of 1965 Jones moved into a new rented home, a mews cottage in Chelsea at 7, Elm Park Lane. Wyman commented that Jones believed it was haunted, no further detail about that was provided however (Wyman, 1997, 306).

The experience of the female spirit voice in Jones's Cotchford Farm cottage was not the only clairaudience (*see glossary*) experience he had. One New Year's Eve year after the band had played a gig at the Lincoln ballroom, Jones, Ian Stewart and another (unnamed) went in the dead of night to visit Lincoln Cathedral. The cathedral was deserted all locked up and there was nobody around except the trio. Suddenly, they all heard the organ playing (Booth, 2012, 148) … *'a long sustained wail. Just one note-very creepy … At least it scared me and the other bloke with us, I remember. It didn't seem to bother Brian'*.

This shows again that Jones had an ease and familiarity with experiences of a supernatural nature. Perhaps he started having psychic encounters at a very young age and so it became the norm to him. Hence him not being bothered by hearing the eerie sound of the church organ coming from inside the locked-up building.

Another example of Jones having the gift of clairaudience and being inspired can be seen by the following example. He told his friend Nicholas Fitzgerald that when he swam in the sea in Tangier that he could hear music in his head, new melodies and new songs (Fitzgerald, 1985, 142). He explained to his friend that *'The colors you wouldn't believe. I love the colors there under the sea. You can't describe it – you have to see it'*.

He knowledgably described to Fitzgerald how Tchaikovsky complained to his nanny about the music that he could hear coming from inside his head, as well as how Beethoven ended up completely deaf. It is believed that the composers last words were *'I shall hear music in heaven'* which Jones said he found extremely sad. Clearly Jones was versed in the lives of these two classical composers as well as sensitive to the loss of hearing that Beethoven lived with, as well as the challenges that Tchaikovsky endured in hearing music in his head that others could not.

Being a musician Jones would have understood the importance of having his hearing and listening faculties working to full optimum. Touring musicians and crew members (as well as DJs) are susceptible to developing hearing disorders which include NIHL (Noise-induced hearing loss) and tinnitus due to their increased exposure to loud sounds, particularly over a long period of time.

When the body is run down, the immune system is weakened, and it becomes easier to become unwell physically and psychologically (Embleton, 2022, 434–445). The latter is pertinent to Jones given how physically weak he already was prior to becoming a touring musician, whether he did develop a hearing disorder we do not know.

Film-maker and occultist Kenneth Anger said that *'Brian was the most psychic of The Stones. He saw the spirit world; for the others it was just the climate of the times. One gets the impression he just dissolved into it'* (Giuliano, 1994, 55). This comment shows that Jones was naturally mediumistic and points to the sensitive and visionary side of his nature and the transcending energy of Neptune. When a subject is mediumistic and psychic and channels that energy, it is extremely important that they have a healthy brain by looking after their mental and physical health as well as their emotional well-being otherwise it can be detrimental all round (Carrington, 1975, X).

Al Aronowitz recollected that one of the first things Jones ever told him about was a vision that he had. The experience took place in London as he was coming out of a London nightclub at approximately 3.00am. He elaborated that *'it was if the heavens had called upon him to look up and see the face of a goddess-angel telling him to work for human good. It was the vision that guided him for as long as I knew him and yet, he always kept cursing himself as one who used his power for evil'* (Giuliano, 1994, 192). He concluded that Jones *'died a man whose vision had somehow carried him into decadence. He died as one of the leaders of a generation that was determined to build the biggest monument to itself in the history of mankind'* (Giuliano, 1994, 193).

Eighteen months after Jones died, Bristol-born mediumistic and sensitive Jacqui Saunders had a vivid communication with Jones's spirit. She recounted that she was lying in bed and saw his face on the wall. *'I sat up and everywhere I looked I could see his face. Knew it wasn't my imagination. Brian came to me because we were so alike … It was an incredible experience for me* (Giuliano, 1994, 197). She continued with confidence *'Brian has taught me not to be afraid of death … He will always guide me through life'* which shows the significant influence that Jones had upon Saunders.

Three days after Jones's death Marianne Faithfull and Mick Jagger were in Australia filming for *Ned Kelly*. Marianne had been prescribed some 'downers' from her doctor as she had a fear of flying. When they reached their hotel room she took the remainder of the tablets and at first was alert and mobile but then started to have some visions. One of which was that as she was looking out of the window, she saw Jones looking up at her from the pavement below and then she fell into a six-day coma (Giuliano, 1994, 186) during which she experienced the following vivid dream. She was walking along with the dead Jones who had woken up in the dream but didn't know where he was. He kept saying to her *'Thank God you're here Marianne'*. The two of them glided along as though they were ice skating their feet not touching the ground. Jones had awoken frightened and lonely not knowing where he was. He was confused and didn't know that he was dead. Faithfull said that in the dream she didn't mind being in that dimension with him.

She believed that when people die quickly that they experience terrible confusion and don't realise they are dead which accounts for why there are ghosts on the earth plane. This was just as Jones had described ghosts to his friend Fitzgerald. She also revealed that she and Jones had conversations whilst he was alive that *'Death is the next great adventure'*. Eventually, Faithfull was awoken from her dream by voices calling her back. Had Jagger not acted swiftly his girlfriend would have passed into the spirit world and would have been there permanently with Jones (Giuliano, 1994, 187).

At the time of writing, Prince Stash told the author that he creates intuitive music and sometimes, when he is in the process of doing so, he senses Jones's spirit around him. Quite possibly he is helping his friend to create. Helping other musicians and singers to create was nothing unusual of him. Just as his parents had taught Jones how to play musical instruments; he was also generous in sharing his knowledge and skills to others who were enthusiastic to learn.

Marianne Faithfull commented that Jones *'was at his best in non-verbal situations, as with the musicians from Jajouka, just playing their instruments together'* and that he *'was at his very best when no words were needed'* (Faithfull, 1994, 246). It is little wonder that his friend Prince Stash should sense Jones around him when he is in a process of creating intuitive music.

Astrologically, we can see this message in his natal chart by way of Jupiter being positioned in Gemini. Jupiter is about enjoyment, teaching and sharing whilst Gemini is about learning and stimulation. For example, (and as previously noted) Jones taught Mick Jagger how to play the harmonica, he also shared *'obscure tunings he'd worked out, especially Open G, learned from Robert Johnson and Muddy Waters and taught it to Keith Richards and Dick Taylor'* (Cooper & Taylor, 2020, an appreciation by Paul Trynka).

Paul Pond remembered how Jones was open-handed to him in teaching him a technique that he had mastered called *'cross harp'* which essentially meant using a harmonica in the *'wrong key'*. Pond remembered that Jones was the first musician on the blues scene to understand and work out that skill. This demonstrates not only his generosity in teaching others and sharing his knowledge but also his determination and tenacity to be able to play a distinctive sound.

Returning to the mystical areas and interest in Jones's life …

Occasionally he would seek advice from fortune-tellers and gurus. Rumour has it that in the Christmas of 1968, while he and his girlfriend Suki Poitier were visiting Ceylon, they went to consult with a fortune teller. Jones was given a strange warning *'Be careful swimming in the coming year. Don't go into the water without a friend'*. The caution gave Jones reason for apprehension and concern as afterwards he always ensured that nobody swam in his swimming pool without supervision (Wohlin, 2005, 100). However seven months later, after the seer's advice, he was dead.

Marianne Faithfull was also a practitioner of the divining arts along with her friend and Jones's girlfriend Anita Pallenberg. On a regular basis they both consulted the I-Ching as well as other forecasting and insightful practices. Faithfull described them as *'the usual hippie stuff'*: Tarot cards, ouija boards and so on' (Faithfull, 1994, 242).

During 1969 Faithfull became increasingly concerned about Jones. She took the I-Ching art seriously and used it to consult on the wellbeing of Jones whom she felt had *'something very nasty coming'*. She consulted the I-Ching early one June evening and got the reading *'Death by Water'*.

Finding the outcome very odd she decided to consult again and received the same result again (Faithfull, 1994, 243).

Such was her concern that she and Mick Jagger decided to phone Jones. They found him in good spirits and he invited them to Cotchford Farm for dinner to which they cordially accepted. However the evening didn't go well and Jagger and Jones fought. This resulted in Jones falling into his moat in the grounds of his estate which put a stop to all the punching and shoving.

Faithfull was hugely relieved believing that the repeated message of 'death by water' shown in the I-Ching must have been of symbolic relevance rather than literal. However, two weeks later she received a phone call from Tom Keylock informing her that Jones had drowned in his swimming pool (Faithfull, 1994, 244).

Suki Poitier who lived at Cotchford Farm prior to Anna Wohlin also had psychic ability. After the car crash in which she survived but Tara Browne, her boyfriend, died (he had separated from his wife Niki), she had a premonition. She told Jim Carter-Fea (a friend of Jones and manager of the Revolution Club in the sixties) that *'she was convinced that three more men who were in close proximity to her would die'* (Hotchner, 1990, 313). Sadly, her prophecy came to fruition.

The three men were Brian Jones, Jimi Hendrix and her husband Robert Ho whom she married in the nineteen seventies. Apparently, the latter told her that he planned to divorce her and she was distraught at the thought of having to return to England alone with their two children. The prospect of this situation disturbed her so much that she drove off a cliff killing both of them. Another account however, describes their final hours as being in Portugal and that they were victims of a fatal hit and run crash, as they were returning home to their two daughters having had dinner with Ho's mother (www.en-academic.com).

In Jones's natal chart the eleventh and ninth houses are occupied by several planets showing a focus in the aforementioned areas. This is pertinent given Jones's psychic abilities and spiritual leanings. This is because the eleventh house associations include futurism and truths (as discussed earlier) whilst ninth house correspondences include belief, cultures, religion, philosophy and vision.

COURAGE, TRADITION & THE UNORTHODOX

Positioned in the ninth house are Mars, Saturn and Uranus. Mars in this area suggests that Jones may have pursued a desire to see the world, held strong philosophical and religious beliefs and was able to defend them if necessary. The confident and optimistic qualities connected with Mars also suggest that he was enthusiastic and unafraid to take risks with any visions that he may have had. An obvious example of this is his solo project outside of *The Stones* music, working with the native Jajoukan musicians in bringing their music to the world and which he posthumously achieved.

Uranus in the ninth house echoes how alternative and unique Jones's work with the group of musicians was during the late 1960s, and, how he become a trailblazer, not only for the blues genre in Great Britain but also for the ethnic music of the Jajouka musicians by bridging different cultures together. Uranus in the ninth house coupled with Mercury in Aquarius also indicates that Jones was a passionate idealist and an independent thinker. Speaking in 1967 he said *'I believe we're moving toward a new age in ideas and events*' (Dalton, 1980, 29).

He revealed some astrological knowledge when he said '*Astrologically, we are at the end of the Pisces age – at the beginning of which people like Christ were born*. The nearing Age of Aquarius Jones believed would hold '*events as important as those at the beginning of Pisces are likely to occur. There's a young revolution in thought and manner about to take place.*

Marianne Faithfull commented that '... *he was convinced there was a mystic link between druidic monuments and flying saucers. Extraterrestrials were going to read these signs from their spaceship windows and get the message*' (Faithfull, 1995, 87). She added that the local credo was all about Glastonbury, ley lines and intelligent life in outer space.

Friend and musician Alexis Korner remembered that '*Brian liked to talk about the fringes of metaphysics ... He was very interested in extrasensory perception, but for very short periods of time* (Aftel, 1982, 93). Korner also observed that Jones was interested in Buddhism but concluded '*I think he was more interested in the paraphernalia than the philosophy. Oh he loved paraphernalia ... He loved the panoply and all the decorations around religion.*

Prince Stash recalled how he and Jones held many a conversation about existentialism and similarly related subjects (Prince Stash in conversation with author). Nicholas Fitzgerald recalled how Jones '*was a man in search of a faith*' (Fitzgerald, 1985, 43). Apparently, his favourite Bob Dylan song which was from the album '*Times They Are a-Changing*' was *With God On Our Side* even though it had bitterly ironic lyrics. It is an anti-war song with a religious element to it. If this was Jones's favourite song it projects something about his moral and political views (subjects also connected with the ninth house).

His principles regarding his status in society and of some of the inequalities globally are evident when he declared in 1967 *'We believe there can be no evolution without revolution. I realise there are other inequalities – the ratio between affluence and reward for work done is all wrong'* (1980, Dalton, 29). Reflecting and with candour, he continued *'I know I earn too much but I'm still young and there's something spiteful inside me which makes me want to hold on to what I've got'*, perhaps the 'something' is his previous experience of poverty before *The Stones* became successful.

Speaking in 1967 Jones stated that *The Stones'* real followers have moved on with them and that one group of people that the band particularly liked *'are the hippies in New York'*. He went on to say how they, like the band were questioning some of the basic immoralities which are tolerated in present day society. He illustrated his position by referencing *'the war in Vietnam, persecution of homosexuals, illegality of abortion and drug taking'* (Dalton, 1980, 29). He also went on to say that he didn't *'underestimate the power or influence of those, unlike me, who do believe in God'*.

Saturn positioned in the ninth house of his natal chart suggests that where philosophy and religion are concerned that he would have wanted definite answers to basic questions concerning the meaning and importance of life. The position also suggests that Jones may have been brought up under repressed or orthodox forms of religion.

This is borne out by the family following a Baptist religion and there is indication of conventional and structured religion in the family heritage by the Sagittarius IC (*see glossary*). The family's beliefs may have felt burdensome, limiting and without meaning to Jones, such is the nature of Saturn and as we heard earlier that, when he was twenty-five years old, he said he did not believe in God. Irrespective of these feelings and thoughts, Jones did have knowledge of the Bible and it's teachings. Anna Wohlin recalled at Cotchford Farm that he would read aloud from it and knew the Old Testament very well and loved to read it. She continued how he had an ability to bring the book alive (Wohlin, 2005, 117).

Mick Martin was Jones's gardener at Cotchford Farm and he was also a lay preacher who ran Sunday Bible classes for the local youngsters. With his calmer outlook on life and as he began to heal from the pounding his body had taken mentally and physically from the drink and drugs, Jones became virtually obsessed with wanting to ensure that nobody took any drugs near him or his home.

He declared enthusiastically to Martin that he wanted to attend the Bible classes and talk to the students warning them about the perils of drink and drugs. He thought they should know that *'my life until now has been rotten. I know it seems to them a world of complete pleasure, but they should know what it's really like'* (Jackson, 1992, 195). It seems that Jones had returned to the 'good book' of conventional religion for clarity and definition and intended to take the platform in the local Bible classes to preach to the children about the dangers of drinking alcohol and using drugs. Whether he ever spoke to Martin's group of pupils we do not know,

Before Jones had returned to the 'good book' in the late nineteen-sixties he had more unorthodox religious leanings and this is indicated by Uranus in the ninth house of his natal chart. This is borne out by his strong interest in Paganism with a special interest in the Greek god Pan. He is the goat-foot god of fertility, nature, the wild, flocks, shepherds and mountain wilds. He played pipes made of reed (hence Pan-Pipes) and was also a passionate pursuer of nymphs. Jones attraction to Pan must have been heightened when he discovered in the early summer of 1968 when visiting Tangier that, the Jajouka villagers' annual festival was the relics of a pre-Roman celebration: The Rites of Pan (Aftel, 1982, 178).

He recorded the event and sent for *Rolling Stones* sound engineer George Chkiantz who assisted him with the project *'Brian Jones Presents the Pipes of Pan at Jajouka'* and which as previously noted was released posthumously by *The Rolling Stones*.

Approximately, every twenty nine years Saturn by transit returns to the natal position in one's birth chart. So, the first Saturn Return occurs when the person is about twenty nine years old and the second Saturn Return happens when he or she is around fifty eight years old. Interestingly, this album was released in the year of Jones's first Saturn Return.

This is an important astrological transit and occurs between the age bracket of twenty eight to thirty one years. It signifies maturity and becoming established and it can mark the end of something and the beginning of something new. Although Jones died before his first Saturn return which would have been when he was twenty nine, the release of the *'Brian Jones Presents the Pipes of Pan at Jajouka'* was considerable. When Saturn returned to the natal ninth house it indicated that Jones had broadened his horizons, had experienced significant life lessons during his travels as well as encountering foreign cultures and embracing their beliefs (see part 3/Fig.3). This album is evidence of this and the sleeve notes that Jones and his colleagues wrote for it help to illustrate this.

Pertinent to Jones's Saturn Return is that this planet is the ruler of Capricorn in astrology. The symbol for this sign is the mountain goat which was pivotal in the narrative about Jones dining with the villagers of Jajouka. So, in Jones's second Saturn return he had established himself as a solo artist and able to work not just with another group but a group from a different culture to his own.

Jimmy Page was a regular visitor to Jones's flat at 1, Courtfield Road where he lived with Pallenberg, at that time Page was still a member of *The Yardbirds*. He commented that Jones *'was into Paganism, Zen, Moroccan tapestries ... and drugs* (Wall, 2008, 215). Marianne Faithfull took sanctuary with the couple at their flat after her marriage to John Dunbar broke down and vividly recalled that in the flat was *'A grotesque little stuffed goat standing on an amp'* (Wells, 2021, 70).

Jones may have been aware that his Moroccan tapestries (and rugs) may have held a divine message as this is something that Islamic cultures geometrically use in some of their exquisite and mysterious patterns. For example, there is a pattern called *'Perfect Fourteen'* which is the number of the prophet, the pattern is based on fourteen-fold rosettes. The Prophet Muhammad is held to be the mirror of Divine Light within creation and is associated with the full moon and the number fourteen (Sutton, 2007, 40).

Acquaintance, and visitor to the flat, Martin Wilkinson recalled how Jones also had an interest in Tibetan Buddhism and the latter had created a Mandela on one of the walls in the Courtfield Road flat. He remembered that *'It was like a picture of his life with all the elements represented in it. It was supposed to represent what your life meant. I remember thinking it was incredibly sinister'* (Howard, 2008, 287). There is a strong artistic tradition in Tibetan Buddhism, this is used as an understanding and ever-present reminder of the spiritual domain in the physical world, examples of the visual aids include paintings, flags, pictures and public prayer wheels (www.bbc.co.uk/).

Marianne Faithfull also commented on Jones's artwork in Courtfield Road, She recalled how *'he began to paint a mural of a graveyard on the wall behind the bed-just above the pillows was a large headstone'* she continued ... *'He never got around to writing his name on it, but you knew the headstone was for him'* (Faithfull, 1995, 93).

Jones and Pallenberg would visit the counterculture Indica Books and Art Gallery (first situated off Duke Street in Mason's Yard and later Southampton Row near the Aldwych) purchasing the latest occult tomes (Wall, 2008, 216). During one shopping spree they purchased *The Golden Dawn* by Israel Regardie and *The Golden Bough* by James George Frazer (Wells, 2021, 71).

Given his interest in Pan and the goat-foot god Jones may also have owned a copy of the novel *The Goat – Foot God* by occultist Dion Fortune which was first published in 1936. The story is about Hugh Paston who converts an old monastery into a temple in order to evolve the goat-foot god, Pan.

The esoteric and occult bookshops *Atlantis* and *Watkins Bookshop* situated in London were (and remain) active in the late 1960s, so possibly Jones and Pallenberg also made trips to those outlets and expanded their book collections, apparently *'the bookshelves at Courtfield Road began to bulge'* (Wells, 2021, 71). Indica was the first UK outlet to stock Timothy Leary's *The Psychedelic Experience* which has been described as a *'DIY manual approach to LSD usage'*.

Jimmy Page remained a loyal friend to Jones long after his friend had split-up with Pallenberg. When he moved out of London to Cotchford Farm, Page regularly visited him at his new home in East Sussex (Wall, 2008, 216). Jones and Page would certainly have made conducive company for each other not only in terms of musicianship, but because Page has been described as having a *'truly encyclopaedia knowledge of the occult, be it of Pagan, Pantheist, Kabbalistic, Masonic, Druidic, or any other esoteric origin'* (Wall, 2008, 214). In the mid-late nineteen seventies and up until 1979, Page owned an occult bookshop and publishing house called *Equinox Booksellers and Publishers* which was at 4 Holland Street, Kensington (www.shadyoldlady.com).

His natal chart has indications of the potential to be interested in the occult (see part 3/Fig.5). He said that he when he was at school, he *'was always interested in alternative religions'* … *'I was always interested in mysticism, Eastern tradition, Western tradition'*. Pallenberg's natal chart also indicates an attraction to the occult. Mick Wall biographer of *Led Zeppelin* wrote that she had an *'enthusiastic but amateurish interest in the occult'* (Wall, 2008, 210), which in comparison to Jimmy Page's extensive occult knowledge may well have been true. Page observed how Pallenberg had a High Priestess aspect about her and was attracted to the occult, and rarely was she without her bag which contained rolling papers, Tarot cards and occasionally the odd bone' (Salewicz, 2018,100).

CROWLEY, GOATS, PAN, BOU JELOUD & THE RITES OF THE JAJOUKA

Pallenberg certainly did have an interest in magic and witchcraft. Her friend Kenneth Anger, who was a filmmaker and occultist, was fascinated by Aleister Crowley and was an adherent of Thelema the religion founded by him. Anger was influential to Pallenberg and her interest in Buddhism, the occult and black magicians (Wells, 2021, 189). Some of her interests would inevitably stimulate Jones too. Velvet Underground singer Nico who had a relationship with Jones said that he read books by Aleister Crowley; she described Crowley as *'an old English man (Aleister Crowley) who was the devil'* (Wells, 2021, 43).

Prince Stash confirmed that Jones was interested in Crowley and *'Especially with psychedelics being involved, there was a definite all-pervading presence of the occult, and its potentiality'* (Trynka, 2014, 165). Anger was convinced that Jones was a form of witch or an 'adept', which he concluded because Jones apparently had a third nipple situated on his inner thigh something also confirmed by one of his lovers (Trynka, 2014, 165).

Interestingly, Jones was friends with film director Donald Cammell who co-directed with Nicolas Roeg, *Performance* which was released in 1970and starred James Fox, Mick Jagger and Anita Pallenberg. His father was Charles Richard Cammell who wrote a biography *'Aleister Crowley, the Black Magician'* which was published in September 1969.

A character called Winona a friend of Jones and Pallenberg recalled how the couple would also visit the Indica gallery and bookshop searching for books of *'Satanic spells to dispel thunder and lightning'* (Wells, 2008, 216). They also held séances at their flat using a Ouija board and other activities included driving out in the middle of the night looking for UFOs.

Pallenberg recalled how she and Brian along with Tara and Niki Browne would *'get in our cars and drive to Staffordshire to look for UFOs. All of us, just lying on a hillside, looking up at the sky. We'd stay up all night then we'd drive back to London'* (Howard, 2016, 239). Pallenberg also said of the two couple's friendship that *'We had loads of affinity together … but the main one was acid'*.

Martin Wilkinson recalled how one day he called to visit Jones at his Courtfield flat. Jones invited him in and said he was teaching Browne the chords on the guitar so that he could learn how to play the blues. He continued that the pair were very, very close (Howard 2016, 286).

Interestingly, the goat featured several times in Jones's life and not just in connection with Paganism. Firstly, as a child when his family kept a goat, *'Neighbours remember him contentedly roaming the pavements with his pet goat, and his inseparable feline companion, Rollader'* (Giulliano, 1994, 3). The latter was a tabby cat and *'they were utterly devoted to each other … he was a child who had a special affinity with animals'* (Jackson, 1992, 3).

His love for animals continued and when he lived at Cotchford Farm he had various cats (names un-known) and two dogs. They were called Emily a black and white cocker spaniel and Luther a black Afghan (Wohlin, 2005, 71). When Jones lived with Linda Lawrence and her family, he bought a goat for them (Jackson, 1992, 91) as well as a white poodle puppy the latter was called Pip (Young, 213, 122).

Lastly, and most significantly regarding the subject of goats featuring in Jones's life, pertains to when he was in the Ahl-Sarif providence of Morocco in the remote village of Jajouka just outside of Tangier. This was in the summer of 1968 he was there with his girlfriend Suki Poitier and his friend the surrealist artist, sound poet and writer Brion Gysin. He lived in Tangier and was part of the Beat generation of the 1950s; he owned a restaurant called *The 1001 Nights.* Gysin knew *The Masters Musicians of Jajouka* as he hired them for entertainment purposes at his eatery. Two other Beats and friends of the *Jajouka* family were author and translator Paul Bowles and visual artist and writer William Burroughs

Jones was an honoured guest of the Jajoukan people and musicians who laid on a great dinner for him; a snow white goat was slaughtered for the occasion. He remembered the goat being killed. Shortly later they were offered the goat's liver on shish kebabs to eat. Jones reacted strongly and said to Gysin *'Now I'm eating my liver'*. Meaning that he identified with the mountain goat as he was the blond man, blond like the goat that had just been killed (Aftel, 1982, 176/177), the scapegoat. After the fulsome meal the musicians performed sections of the night-long ritual of *Pan Bou Jeloud, the Father of Skins especially* for Jones. Chkiantz observed that Jones was in good health and spirits that day, He smoked kif and although he took morphine and asthma medication with him to the village he didn't need to use them (Aftel, 1982, 181). He commented that *'Brian was fascinated; here he was recording genuine folklore* (Aftel, 1982, 179).

Gysin described the rites and music of Jajouka in the notes for Jones's album, *'Magic calls itself The Other Method for controlling matter and space. In Morocco, magic is practiced more assiduously than hygiene though, indeed, ecstatic dancing to music of the brotherhoods may be called a form of psychic hygiene'* (Aftel, 1982, 181). His description continued and further explained that when *Pan Bou Jeloud* danced in the eight moonlit nights in the village that *'a faint breath of panic borne on the wind'* (Aftel, 1982, 182), thus illustrating the nature of dread and fright associated with Pan. He dances to the wailing of his hundred Master Musicians. All the villagers dressed in best white, swirl in great circles and coil around one Wildman in skins' (Gysin, sleeve notes *Jajouka* 1995, POINT, CD album). Paul Bowles wrote that *'When the new moon, before setting, announces that the month-long fast of Ramadan is at an end; the villagers of Jajouka know that Bou Jeloud will be among them that night'* (Bowles, sleeve notes *Jajouka* 1995, POINT, CD album).

William Burroughs described how *Pan, Bou Jeloud* dances in a little square lit by bonfire whilst dressed in black goatskins, as he does so he snatches up branches to whip the women who run screaming before him. The Jajoukan folklore dictates that if he touches a woman with a branch that she will become pregnant before the year is out (Burroughs, sleeve notes *Jajouka* 1995, POINT, CD album).

Jones also wrote sleeve notes for the album. He explained how the village Jajouka was without a road and so transport as well as other comforts such as electricity and plumbing and that in that sense Jajouka was primitive. He commented that *'all knowledge and culture is passed down from mother to child until the age of twelve, at which age the father-community watches over the tender years of the boys and the young girls are not further to be seen until they are married off'* (Jones, sleeve notes *Jajouka* 1995, POINT, CD album).

Commenting on the chants and the women's lead singer, he informs the reader that she had a beautiful voice and that the group were chanting an incantation to those of another plane thus showing the ethereal component in their ritual. Jones finalises by saying *'Anyway, we hope we have captured the spirit and magic of Jajouka'*.

Previously to working with the Master Musicians and villagers of Jajouka, he had been hypnotised by the insistent rhythms of the G'naoua brotherhood and taped them when they were playing in the great square of Marrakesh (Palmer, 1984, 136). He was particularly attracted to the G'naoua black Moroccans whose ancestors had been carried north across the Saharan desert as slaves from the West African coastal region. At that time the territory was suffering the depredation of American and English slavers around the same period (Palmer, 1984, 142).

Story has it that the G'naoua healed the physically sick and cured mental illness with their kinetic drumming and hypnotic click clack of their castanets. When they played their three stringed lutes, they sounded like primitive Mississippi bluesmen. One can see why Jones would have been interested in this group of musicians. He decided to tape a G'naoua rhythm track and overdub a black American soul band on top of it with the intention of then adding Moroccan trance rhythms to *The Stones* music. Sadly, the tape did not record as well as Jones would have liked. Then Gysin took him to the Rif foothills to get to Jajouka. Fortunately, Jones found the Jajoukan music even more powerful than the G'naoua music.

Returning to the astrology and addressing Neptune's house position in Jones's natal chart ...

Astrologer and author Howard Sasportas interpreted that with Neptune in the first house *'Illness at an early age could further accentuate the tenuous hold they have on life in their bodies'* (Sasportas, 1985, 288). This is pertinent to Jones as we already know that he had croup when he was four years old which left him with asthma for the remainder of his life. Sasportas also wrote of those with Neptune in the first house *'A few may turn to hard drugs and alcohol in an attempt to alleviate the harsher realities of life and find themselves worse off in the end'* (Sasportas, 1985, 287), which we know to be true of Jones.

ADAPTABILITY, ILL-HEALTH & MEDICAL ASTROLOGY

The Sun is in the sixth house of his natal chart the area associated with health, service and work and is close to the descendant, we know that ill-health and being employment-shy (outside of being a musician!) was prevalent in Jones's life. Certainly, he could not maintain the daily grind and drudgery of toil and labour. Examples of his many jobs include bus conductor, optician's assistant and carpet salesman.

The four mutable (*see glossary*) signs are positioned at the axis comprising of Virgo (ASC), Sagittarius (IC), Pisces (DC) and Gemini (MC). These points on the axis represent the self, family and heritage, significant partnerships and career and vocation respectively. The vast mutable energy on the axis indicates that Jones was curious and needed relentless stimulation, was analytical, had tremendous self-belief and may have been easily overwhelmed. The latter perhaps being due to the anxiety provoking and energy sapping force created by Mercury the ruler of Gemini and Virgo. Astrologer and author Jane Ridder-Patrick observed that *'Mutable diseases are those of distraction-irrational fears, nervousness and irritability'* (Ridder-Patrick, 1990, 28).

Each of the mutable signs react in their own unique way when presented with a stimulus and this is borne out in the following way. Gemini is curious for the sake of interest, Virgo would find a practical use for it, and Sagittarius would enthuse about it as well as experience and evangelize it. Finally, Pisces accepts without any questioning as being part of the universal whole.

Jones's natal chart is dominated by planets in the fixed (*see glossary*) signs comprising of: Moon, Pluto in Leo, Mercury, Venus in Aquarius and finally Mars, Saturn and Uranus in Taurus. Such type of energy would help to concentrate and stabilise the flowing and meandering nature of the mutable vigour. He could indeed be determined and persevering when he wanted to be. The obvious example being in creating a blues band whose members rebelliously grew their hair long and performed blues music in Great Britain which was anarchic and revolutionary at the time. Despite all the challenges, Jones succeeded in turning his dreams into a reality showing his capacity to be resolute and unwavering.

The fleeting and restless energy of the MC (*see glossary*) Gemini is exacerbated by the Sun in Pisces square MC and suggests that Jones was likely to have multiple careers and interests, Astrologer and author Frank C. Clifford observed that for those with MC Gemini in a creative job *'the professional name (or nickname) might differ from our birth name, and we enjoy dual personas or some other split between our private and public selves'* (Clifford, 2016, 27). This is certainly borne out

WHAT BRIAN JONES'S NATAL CHART REVEALS

by Lewis Brian Hopkin Jones calling himself *'Elmo Lewis'* and *'Brian Jones'*.

A recent documentary aired on the BBC *The Stones and Brian Jones* by director Nick Broomfield shows archives of Jones being interviewed in the nineteen-sixties. He was asked by the interviewer what he was doing before he became a Rolling Stone. He replied *'just bumming around waiting for something to happen really'* (Broomfield, 2023, Magnolia Pictures).

He certainly didn't have any problems in securing employment as jobs were plentiful then but due to the roles not being stimulating enough and because he had a bigger plan for himself, he was unable to maintain a job. He took jobs while he was in-between touring for financial purposes. Work that offered mobility, short-term commitments and the freedom to travel would have been more appealing to him. This was certainly fulfilled by his work as a touring musician; at least it was in the earlier years of his life as a *Stone*.

Given that *The Rolling Stones* have been playing for over sixty years now, had Jones still been alive and interested in the type of music that the band is playing, one cannot help but wonder if he would have become bored, with the evergreen routine of world touring. In all probability he would have. At the time of writing the band have announced their next global circuit for 2024 called the *Hackney Diamonds* tour (https://rollingstones.com/tour/).

Sun positioned in the sixth house also indicates that Jones needed to be proud of the work that he did whilst bringing a valuable contribution to society. However, what was valuable to him may not have been perceived by others in society as important, either in the nineteen sixties or in contemporary times. In the 1960s he was interviewed and asked about the screaming *Rollin' Stones* fans in Sydney when they first played there. He declared that *'you feel a personal pride'* (Broomfield, 2023, Magnolia Pictures) reflecting upon their success in Australia and how their music was much valued there.

His irrepressible drive and vision was to perform and play in a blues band which he achieved but, sadly, his part in it came to an end when he was just twenty seven years old. The band he formed named and played with asked him to leave the group in June 1969. Just one month later he was dead. Jones's death certificate recorded his occupation and usual address as *Entertainer, Cotchford Farm Hartfield* (Guiliano, 1994, 258).

The Sun is square (*see glossary*) Jupiter in his natal chart and indicates that he pushed himself to excess through immoderation and self-indulgence which was essentially the cause of many of his physical problems. Charlie Watts confirmed Jones's immoderation when he said *'Brian was one of those people who did everything to excess'* (Broomfield, 2023, Magnolia Pictures).

In her book *Medical Astrology* astrologer and author Wanda Sellar observed that with the Sun square Jupiter aspect that *'Over indulgence may bring liver problems'* (Sellar, 2008, 120). Her observation is illustrated whereby on Jones's death certificate which was registered on the 9th July 1969, the cause of his death was recorded as *'Drowning, Immersion in Fresh Water severe liver dysfunction due to fatty degeneration and the ingestion of alcohol and drugs. Swimming whilst under the influence of alcohol and drugs. MISADVENTURE* (Guiliano, 1994, 258). The notes from the post-mortem examination at the Queen Victoria Hospital, East Grinstead on 3rd July

WHAT BRIAN JONES'S NATAL CHART REVEALS

1969 state that Jones was *'powerfully built, with a tendency to obesity'* (Guiliano, 1994, 252).

Sun positioned in the sixth house also indicates that health and ill-health may have been a focus throughout Jones's life and indeed it was. The Sun is opposite the Virgo ascendant in his natal chart and this sign is ruled by Mercury. In medical astrology Mercury represents nervous sensitivity and mental ability as well as ruling the voice box, vocal cords and the tongue. The planet's energy also influences (amongst other things): the breath, lungs, bronchi and trachea as well as arms, fingers, hands and shoulders. Associated Mercury health conditions some of which are pertinent to Jones include; asthma, breathing disorders, cholera, and epilepsy, and insomnia, mental and nervous problems as well as panic attacks. Dick Hattrell claimed that Jones *'was under a psychiatrist's care for years. There was always a sense of doom about him'* (Giuliano, 1994, 194).

Talking therapy has been in existence since Freud started it in the eighteen nineties with his revolutionary psychoanalysis. Many of his theories seem to have informed Jones's psychiatric assessments during his lifetime.

Whilst the middle of the twentieth century saw a rise in pharmaceutical interventions (both prescription and non-prescription), to help manage the Nations mental health, during the last thirty years or so, there has been some balance restored. This has been through the steady rise in the variety and accessibility of talking therapies. What was once seen as shameful and pathologising delinquency, psychiatric illness and learning disability, has become more open and discussed, with more emphasis on holistic wellbeing as well as celebrating neurodiversity.

Linda Lawrence recalled how Jones used to become agitated and worried about his visits home and that as he got nearer, he would have an asthma attack. He used to make sounds as if he was going to vomit and he had to use his inhaler, Lawrence also carried an inhaler in case Jones lost his (Aftel, 1982, 58). He was beleaguered with severe asthma from early childhood right up until his death. The asthma attacks would plague him when he was unusually excited. When he lived in Windsor, Berkshire with Lawrence, he could have asthma attacks as often as three times a week. As Jones got older the attacks happened virtually on a daily basis. Experiencing an asthma attack can generate a brutal succession *'it causes panic and a sensation of near-death by suffocation; that experience reinforces a feeling of anxiety, solitude, and fear'*. Today, severe asthma is considered a disability under the Equality Act (www.asthmaandlung.org.uk/).

Jones's lifestyle did little to aid his health. As his anxieties about the band's apparent take-over by Jagger and Richards grew, his addictive cigarette smoking grew to approximately sixty daily (Reed, 1999, 47) which would have greatly exacerbated his asthma. *Kent* was one of several brands that he smoked. He also began to rely on alcohol for his nerves and developed a taste for brandy, whisky and Bacardi and Coke. No doubt *The Stones* relentless tour schedule would have meant that Jones was reliant largely on junk food that was snatched in between shows. This would have meant that his body had little chance to detox.

Valium was prescribed to Jones right up until his death as confirmed by his doctor who reported that his patient *'needed all of the time'* (Guiliano, 1994 *Sudden Death-Brian Jones doc*). This is interesting in that Valium is also prescribed for seizures as well as anxiety (www.amfmtreatment.com/). Jones's doctor advised that the Valium was for purposes of being a tranquiliser so to reduce his anxiety.

His close friend Prince Stash commented and observed that *'It was really really tragic with Brian because downers make you lose your ability and he lost musical ability, considerable musical ability'* (Houghton, 2015, 271). Ian Stewart (the sixth Rolling Stone) agreed with Lawrence that Jones was *'a very unhealthy person'* and that *'he was allergic to a lot of things'*. Interestingly, allergies are also associated with Virgo Jones's ascendant sign. As well as carrying an inhaler with him Jones also carried some pills which were probably antihistamines.

After Jones's death a report from his doctor Dr. A.L. Greenburgh showed that Jones had recently put in a request for regular prescriptions for a Medihaler as well as *Piriton* to help manage his hay-fever. Greenburgh also confirmed that Jones was regularly prescribed: *Mandrex* (as sleeping tablets, 2 to 3 per day), *Valium* -10 mg as tranquilisers, 3 per day which he needed all of the time and *Durophet* (aka *'black bombers'*) which were infrequently prescribed (Giuliano, 1994, doc: *Sudden Death-Brian Jones*).

Linda Lawrence recalled how Jones seemed *'to be allergic to a lot of the standard sort of pills you get for this'* and on one occasion he had to visit the hospital because somebody had given him some pills *'and his skin was literally falling off his arms'* (Aftel, 1982, 58). Keith Richards speaking after Jones's death said that he knew he was asthmatic and how *'he was hung up on his spray'* (Hotchner, 1990, 318). Unsurprisingly really, given that his spray was a lifeline to him.

The perceptive Bill Wyman had another inclination about Jones's ill-health and which gives some explanation and insight as to some of Jones's unpredictable behaviour and ill-health. The reason being that Jones may have been living with undiagnosed epilepsy. Wyman came to this conclusion having befriended one of Jones's illegitimate daughters who was unknown to her father (born in 1960) and who wanted to remain anonymous. She revealed to Wyman that she had temporal-lobe epilepsy and believed that she may have inherited the epileptic symptoms from Jones (Wyman & Coleman, 1997, 175).

Jones's daughter explained that when she has the fits that she goes straight into a collapse with no warning signs, often they occur during the middle of the night. Her parents would know about it but she would be oblivious as she would have had the fit and gone straight to sleep. This concurs with an incident that happened to Jones in approximately 1967. He was in Marrakesh staying at a hotel with girlfriend Suki Poitier and George Chkiantz.

The three of them were on their hotel balcony when *'Brian suddenly keeled over. He had blacked out'* (Wyman & Havers, 2002, 308). This was a shock to Chkiantz but Poitier told him that it was a regular occurrence and assured him that Brian would be alright if he slept for a while. Putting him on the bed and allowing him to sleep, when he eventually awoke he told them he remembered nothing of what happened.

Wyman told Jones's daughter how her father was *'permanently worried about his health ... He did seem to suffer sudden depressions and swings of mood'* (Wyman& Coleman, 1997, 175). The daughter explained to Wyman about her seizures *'They can make you feel really ill; you don't know what's going on. It would mean he wouldn't be able to carry on a proper conversation with people. Your brain suddenly goes thud. You've had it'.* She continued that if Jones didn't know that he had epilepsy and was coming round how it *'felt bloody awful, like sawdust, in the morning … then maybe Brian felt he had a hangover. There's no cure, but tablets or drugs can control it'* (Wyman & Coleman, 175, 1997).

According to Wyman, Jones found stage work hard because of his asthma. Whilst he loved the fame the pressure got to him. He observed that *'The emotional drain of a performance sometimes got him so worked up that he looked dangerously exhausted at the end'* (Wyman & Colman, 1997, 209). Wyman added that *'Perhaps because of that inner tension and fear of an attack while he played, he promoted the most unsmiling, insolent image of all five of us. This made him even more attractive to the girls'*. In October 1965 fan Pauline Gerrard went to see *The Stones* at the Granada Theatre in Tooting. She recalled that *'the loudest outburst came when Brian Jones was introduced – sultry smiling, hair flopping over his eyes. Every female in the audience immediately fell in love with the broody guy* (Houghton, 2015, 239/240). Her description captures what Wyman said of Jones's stage impression of insolence.

It was not unusual for Jones to be late for shows, miss recording sessions, concerts and, rehearsals on the grounds of ill-health and sometimes for very serious reasons like being hospitalised. For example, Jones was admitted into hospital when he was in the USA and supposed to appear on stage in Milwaukee. However, he was admitted to hospital after a hotel doctor had to give him a sedative and found that his temperature was 105 degrees.

Hospital doctors diagnosed that Jones was suffering from bronchitis and extreme exhaustion; he became delirious and had to be fed intravenously (Wyman& Colman, 1997, 279). Another fan, Jo Poole went to see the group in 1963 and recalled how she *'was dreadfully upset when Brian Jones turned up late and was not on stage at the start of the show'* (Houghton, 2015, 47).

Another fan Estelle Fowden recalled on a different occasion how after seeing the band play that she went to the stage door and asked Jones for his autograph. *'I can see his face now, very pale and drawn with big bags under the eyes. He didn't look at all healthy for a young bloke'* (Houghton, 2015, 71). Certainly, Jones was experiencing ill-health as Fowden observed and it continued throughout his lifetime.

In 1985 Pallenberg described Jones as being *'a tortured personality, insecure as hell. He was ill very early on from when I met him. He was totally paranoiac'* adding that *'I think Brian was a terrible person really … And I put up with a lot'* (Balfour, 1986, 117).

His continued drug use as well as self-loathing and paranoia led to several suicide attempts of which Jones's chauffeur, Brian Palastanga claims to have witnessed two of the aborted suicide attempts (Giulliano, 1994, 80). One was when Jones was staying at the Royal Garden Hotel and climbed to the window ledge threatening to throw himself off the top of the building. Palastanga tackled Jones and managed to get inside the hotel. Another occasion involved him and Jones driving along the Embankment in London and whereby, the latter scaled the wall and threatened to jump into the Thames, he implored *'Please help me'*.

When Jones stood for his appeal in December 1967 following his conviction in the September of 1967, an independent psychiatrist Professor Walter Neustatter was used by the court to provide a profile on Jones. His detailed report included that in his considered opinion *'Mr Jones is, at present, in an extremely precarious state of emotional adjustment as a result of his unresolved problems with aggressive impulses and sexual identification'* (Giulliano, 1994, 73).

The Professor also reported that whilst Jones's current anxiety was centred on the prospect of him being sent to prison that *'its underlying resources are more deeply rooted ... Indeed, it is very likely that his imprisonment could precipitate a complete break with reality, a psychotic breakdown and significantly increase the suicidal risk for this man'*.

These health examples and references evidence astrologically how the Sun in the sixth house and in opposition to Virgo the ascendant sign, coupled with the Sun square Jupiter manifested on both his mental and physical health on a daily basis.

FAME & THE BLUES

Sun square Jupiter coupled with the Sun square the MC also reveals (aside from his medical issues) that Jones was ambitious and determined, could and did work hard to achieve his vision and be influential once he got there. Jupiter positioned in the tenth house is an indicator of thriving on being in the public eye, being successful and achieving fame and prominence. Before Jones found prominent recognition with *The Rollin' Stones* he was adamant *'Yes, I will be famous.*

No, I won't make thirty' (Davis, 2002, 4), showing, his confidence and determination as well as an eerie inner knowing about his life being short lived.

Keith Richards recalled part of a conversation with Jones and which appears in *'Blown Away, The Rolling Stones and the Death of the Sixties'* by A.E. Hotchner published in 1990. Richards said *'There are some people who you know aren't going to get old. Brian and I agreed that he, Brian wouldn't live very long. I remember saying "You'll never make thirty" and he said I know'* (Hotchner, 1990, 28).

Accomplishing something momentous in his life which he could be proud of and standing out from the crowd was important to Jones. If he couldn't be a star in his family then he was going to be a VIP in society. This was evident in his short life where as we already know he formed, named and played with the generation influencing British blues, *The Rollin' Stones*.

The band covered and recorded many versions of songs made by American black blues singers in 1964 (although not only confined to that year). During and following their tour of North America, Jones was able to meet some of his heroes such as Chuck Berry and Muddy Waters.

The latter said of Jones *'That guitar player ain't bad'* whilst Chuck Berry said of the group *'Swing on gentlemen, you are sounding most well, if I may so'*. (Wyman & Havers, 2002, 129). Jones's long-time friend Dick Hattrell said Jones *'had the negro superstition and wore a black cat's bone round his neck. In spirit, he would play music like a negro and in spirit he became one'* (Giuliano, 1994, 194).

Other artists (aside from Berry & Walters) who had some of their work covered by the band include: Jimmy Reed,

Irma Thomas, The Valentinos and Howlin' Wolf. Footage of the mainstream American TV programme *Shindig* in May 1965 shows Jones being interviewed. As his interviewed concluded, his excitement was palpable as he went on to joyfully introduce Howlin' Wolf to the studio and television audience (Broomfield, 2023, Magnolia Pictures). Then he sat at the blues singer's feet and watched him perform.

Blues guitarist and singer Buddy Guy recalled how that episode of the show broke through *'a boundary line that could not be crossed'* and Blues writer Peter Guralnick described it as *'as being one of the most significant moments in cultural history'* (Cooper & James, 2020, page heading *'He was the most gifted'*). This shows how liberating and progressive Jones and the *Shindig* programme was in merging different cultures and races together which was quite revolutionary at the time.

By releasing this genre of music, Jones and the rest of his band helped to give the artists wider coverage in America and in the UK, which ultimately gave them greater recognition and success thanks to a largely white teenage generation of Blues fans. Folk singer Donovan who was prominent in the nineteen sixties (who married Linda Lawrence after she and Jones split) observed how The American Blues masters recognised and credited Jones for bringing their music to larger audiences. Bo Diddley said that *'only Brian mastered the Diddley guitar style'* (Cooper& James, 2020, Donovan, Ireland 2019) which is a huge acknowledgement and tribute.

Recording engineer and record producer Glyn Johns recalled that in 1963 when he met the band for the first time, how *'Brian was very much concerned about the sounds that I would produce on tape, He wanted the Jimmy Reed-type sound, which was virtually unheard of in England'* (Wyman & Havers,

2002, 49). He also observed how Jones *'controlled their sound in intimate detail'* (Cooper & James, 2020, an appreciation by Paul Trynka). Whilst Johns had enormous admiration and respect for Jones, as a musician, he did not like him as a person stating *'I took an instant dislike to him, which was to remain for some years'* (Johns, 2015, 43).

Returning once again to the astrology …

KINDRED SPIRITS & SECURITY IN NUMBERS

The Moon in Leo is associated with drama and from what we know of Jones's short life it was full of commotion, spectacle and crisis. When things weren't going his way, his pride may have been easily injured which may have resulted in emotional fireworks in order to cover up any self-doubts he may have had. Moon is positioned in the eleventh house the area associated with friends, groups, kindred spirits and projects.

This is an ideal position for nurturing bands and groups of people; it also suggests security in numbers as well as an instinctive feel for being at home in a troupe dynamic. Bo Diddley said of Jones in the earlier days of *The Stones* that *'he was a little dude that was trying to pull the group ahead. I saw him as the leader. He didn't take no mess. He was a fantastic cat who handled the group beautifully'* (www.brianjonesblues.co.uk), which captures the aforementioned interpretation of the Moon in the eleventh house.

Not only did Jones conceive and develop *The Rollin' Stones* he also played with bands such as *The Beatles* (he played alto saxophone on *You Know My Name (Look Up The Number)*, and *All You Need Is Love*. He was pivotal with the Jajouka tribe and the production of *The Masters of Jajouka* music which contributed widely to world music and still does today.

He recorded the Morocco based ensemble the Master Musicians of Jajouka which was later used by The Rolling Stones in 1971 and was released as *'Brian Jones Presents the Pipes of Pan at Joujouka'* as discussed earlier. Towards the end of his life, he had a concept for a new band whereby he wanted the group members to play a variety of genres of music.

Jones with his eyes lit up at the thought of it told his friend Nicholas Fitzgerald, *'The band I'm forming will play a combination of trad jazz, rhythm and blues, gospel and Moroccan music. A bit of a mixture. But it will work, I know it will'* (Fitzgerald, 1985, 18). Clearly Jones's taste in music had changed and was not confined to traditional jazz and rhythm and blues. In the late 1960s he developed a passion for the American groups *Credence Clearwater Revival* (especially the song *'Bad Moon Rising'*) and *The Lovin' Spoonful* (particularly the track *'Do You Believe In Magic'*).

Jerry Shirley then drummer of the band *Humble Pie* said there had been talk about Jones joining his band after he left *The Rolling Stones*. Jones was meant going to Ongar, Essex on the 2nd July for a jam to see if he could join the group (presumably as well as also having his own new group). Tragically, he remained at home choosing *'to go for a late-night swim instead. Sad but true'* (Spence, 2021, 147/148), things may well have been very different had Jones kept to his original arrangement.

Returning to the subject of the Moon in the eleventh house…

This area also indicates that Jones had many acquaintances who shared a common interest, and whilst he had many contacts there probably were 'hangers-on' and sadly few and genuine friends in his life. This is symbolised through the changing and fluctuating energy of the Moon in the eleventh house. Pat Andrews said of Jones in approximately 1964 that *'he could never have true friends'* (www.youtube.com/PatAndrews). Andrews observations from then were also echoed by Jones's father in 1970 after slowly trying to come to terms with his son's death. Mr Jones commented *'He was naive to the point that he trusted everybody. He was surrounded by people whom he thought were his own friends for his own sake. When he found out that a lot of them could be disregarded as hangers-on, he was most deeply upset'* (Giuliano, 1994, 195).

Returning again to the astrology ...

Pluto is in the eleventh house and shows that Jones could occupy a position of power within the band and use his strength to motivate groups and potentially change society for the better. This is borne out by his determination and passion for *'The Stones'* to play and sing blues. In doing so he was hugely influential in helping to bring to the fore this genre of music in Britain. It was at a time when blues records had been difficult to buy and when playing blues was confined to small clubs and pubs.

Transformation and the taboo are areas associated with Pluto so it could be argued that Jones used his power through his group to bring some of the (then taboo) subjects to the fore. Some examples being racial inequality, poverty and sex themes, which are alluded to in many blues songs. His influence helped to give the blues genre and black artists more coverage and recognition after the *Stones* covered many blues and rhythm and blues tracks which in turn helped them become more successful. Certainly, Jones's band played a pivotal role in the counter culture movement that was happening in Great Britain in the 1960s. Lewis Jones said of his son in 1970 *'All I can say is that I think Brian played his part in shaping the world as it is today'* (Giuliano, 1994, 195).

Paul Trynka described Jones's major contribution in transforming genres of *'The blues and world music he championed has become mainstream, his distinct sonic textures inspired a generation, while his very image, of the aggressive, androgynous peacock male, has become a staple of youth culture'* (Cooper & James, 2020, an appreciation Paul Trynka).

The band's music and legendary performances defined a generation. Today *The Rolling Stones* play to sold out stadiums and they remain as creative and original. In October 2023 they released *Hackney Diamonds* their 24th British and 26th American studio album. It is their first album in eighteen years and made number one in the charts in the UK and another five countries as well being in the top three in the USA. Indeed, a truly outstanding achievement for a band that has been together for more than six decades, thus demonstrating how music, performance and song writing remain the at the core of *The Rolling Stones*.

LOSING CREATIVE CONTROL, SEEKING ATTENTION & UNPREDICTABILITY

Jones felt that he was losing his power as leader of the *Stones* when manager Andrew Loog Oldham wanted to take the band in a different direction. He wanted Jagger and

Richards to write pop songs for the group, believing it was no longer viable to constantly release blues/rhythm and blues cover versions. He wanted Jagger and Richards to become songwriters like Lennon and McCartney believing it would bring more financial success. This was the death of Jones's band and his creative control as he had known it; he had no say in the transformation.

The Moon in Leo energy adds warmth, dazzle and exuberance so it is possible that Jones may have seen himself as a larger than life figure at times, a theme also echoed by the Sun square Jupiter aspect. At times Jones may have deliberately gone overboard and pushed the boundaries seeking attention as indeed Bill Wyman observed.

When Anita Pallenberg filmed *A Degree of Murder* in Munich in 1966 Jones flew out to join her. A publicity photographer took images of them; Jones was dressed in a Nazi S.S. uniform. Unsurprisingly, the photos stirred up controversy and he exacerbated the matter by stating *'These are going to be realistic pictures … The meaning of it all is there is no sense to it'* (Wyman & Havers, 2002, 249) which leads to the question why on earth did he do it?

Bill Wyman commented that *'Sometimes he would do the most stupid things that he instinctively knew would land him in trouble with the press … It was attention seeking in part'*. Wyman concluded that it was Jones's frustration and unhappiness in the band spurred him on to increasingly disparaging conduct.

Mercury in Aquarius along with the Moon opposing Mercury suggests that at times Jones could be shocking, unpredictable, had changeable moods and may have found it challenging to be objective and rational. Keith Richards said of him *'Such a beautiful cat, man. He was one of those people who are so beautiful in one way, and such an asshole in another'* (Dalton, 1980, 28) whilst Mick Jagger said *'there were terrible periods when everyone was against Brian which was stupid but then on the other hand Brian was a very difficult person to get on with and he didn't help'* (Dalton, 1980, 29).

Dawn Molloy experienced the full range of Jones's moodiness at a time when his drug abuse started to worsen. She recalled how *'his dark moods were becoming more and more difficult to decipher and deal with'* (Dawn Young, 2013, 125). His moods included him being calm, angry and distant, brooding and silent. Yet at other times he could be childish, relaxed and silly.

By the time Jones had met Pallenberg in 1965 he was apparently smelling of and consuming two bottles of brandy a day. Alcohol worsened his tenuous disposition, which often lead to meltdowns and tantrums (Winder, 2023, 5/6). However, Pallenberg said that she *'liked Brian's mercurial nature-moody was better than boring in her book. He'd quickly shake off the doom and snap back to his jaunty self'* (Winder, 2023, 6).

Marianne Faithfull recalled from the latter nineteen sixties of Jones that *'He would test levels of endurance, and no one had any patience left. He did it all the time, endlessly. For Brian, relations with other people always took place in the extreme'* (Faithfull, 1995, 245). Anna Wohlin, who lived with Jones in the last year of his life, wrote in her autobiography that *'He was impulsive and unpredictable'* (Wohlin, 2005, 164). Pat Andrews, mother to Jones's son Julian Mark Andrews who was born in 1961 said of Jones *'the kind of person he is he could never be happy ... he is so cynical he's got no feelings for anybody'* (www.youtube.com/Pat Andrews).

INTENSITY, LOSS OF FREEDOM, GRIEF & SORROW

The Moon is in opposition to Venus in the natal chart suggesting that Jones may have found it difficult to take criticism, was very sensitive and could feel rejected and hurt all too easily. One example of this can be seen in his own words Jones was aware of his own susceptive nature stating *'I'm a pretty sensitive sort of person, I always have been. When the Stones are knocked, I feel it personally'* (Wyman & Havers, 2002, 161). His friend Nicholas Fitzgerald commented that *'Brian couldn't seem to comprehend that other people had their own problems, and when they hinted as much he was hurt, assuming they didn't care about him'* (Giuliano, 1994, 96).

This aspect also indicates potential for an intense emotional nature. If he endeavoured to put his demands on others it may have created challenges for him. It also suggests that he may have avoided involvement with others, fearing the responsibility of emotional attachment. This is borne out in the natal chart by Venus in the fifth house the area associated with children and romance, whilst Pluto is positioned in the eleventh house and connected with estrangement and freedom.

Saturn positioned in the ninth house is also an indicator of Jones's fear of losing his freedom. This was something he experienced for a very short while when the authorities imprisoned him for one night in 1968 at HM Prison Wormwood Scrubs. He was released the following day to await appeal in December coming close to serving six months in prison *'the experience left a marked impression on him'* (Giuliano, 1994, 72). The event must have tested him greatly as it would anyone who had lost their liberty.

Mars in the ninth house can also be interpreted as fighting for his freedom. This was certainly borne out not only by the conflict with authority figures, but also striving for privacy away from his invasive fans in order to be free to live a private life like anybody else. Keith Richards described the prison as *'a medieval dungeon from the days of the Borgias'* and that *'Jones had been roughed up pretty good'*. Apparently, one of the prison officers sneered *'We finally got one of those bloody long hairs'* and they threatened to give him a haircut.

Returning to Jones's intense nature and sensitivity, it is possible that these feelings began in his early childhood when his mother emotionally distanced herself from her son after her daughter Pamela died. Louisa Jones may have been living with grief and trauma which may have explained some of her detachment from Lewis Brian. The loss of a child is the most painful and traumatic experiences a parent can go through.

Astrology offers some insight as to the pain and suffering that Jones suffered after his sister Pamela died and possibly leading up to her death. Transiting Pluto was conjunct his natal Moon and Chiron (see Part 3/Fig.2). Associations of Pluto include: crisis, death (both metaphysical and physical), intensity and devastation. The third house ruler in Jones's natal chart the area which governs siblings is governed by Pluto.

Needless to say, as a child and throughout his lifetime too, he was exceptionally sensitive to atmospheres, undercurrents and moods. He may have been receiving intuitive and physical signals, such as body language, lack of eye contact and affection from his mother, indicating that she was suffering with severe despair and sorrow. This may have been over a period of time too leading up to Pamela's death from leukaemia (see part 3/Fig.2.)

Being so young he would not have understood exactly what was going on. Other associations connected with Pluto include concealment, darkness and silence. Babysitter and family friend Trudy Baldwin who knew the Jones family at the time when Pamela died recalled that, his family were friendly but reserved most notably when they lost their daughter. The tragedy they never revealed (Cooper & James, 2020, Trynka appreciation).

However, Jones confided in Baldwin about the secret and she said *'it must have been awful, to hide something like that away'*. The situation shows the Pluto energy in action through the suppression and cover-up of the death of his sister. This must have been a bewildering and intense time for Jones and his parents but especially for him as a toddler. When Mr and Mrs Jones tragically lost their son some twenty four years later after their daughter had died they must have felt overwhelming grief and pain. Dawn Molloy commented that Jones's mother never got over the loss of losing Pamela and *'it seemed that Brian had suffered from her death as well'* (Young, 2013, 70).

In Jones's natal chart the Moon (which represents care giving and nurturing) is conjunct the small planet Chiron which in astrology symbolises 'the wounded healer'. It indicates one's core wounds and can help one realise their deepest inner traumas, whether Jones ever realised this we do not know for certain. In all probability it was unlikely given the vast therapy that he underwent in his later years.

Astrologer and author Melanie Reinhart observed that those with the position of Chiron in Leo may *'have had their spontaneity crushed in childhood and are hypersensitive to ridicule'* (Reinhart, 1989, 126). Interestingly, Jones revealed in a *Rolling Stones* magazine interview that *'my mother thought I was ridiculous, but what can she say now, with all this money rolling in?'* which shows contempt and haughtiness towards his mother about his financial success (Wyman & Havers, 2002, 104). Mandy Aftel perceived that *'Brian's parents were only able to respond favourably to him as he became more successful'* (Aftel, 1983, 60).

In his last years at Cotchford Farm Jones found a maternal bond with his housekeeper Mrs Mary Hallett, and who Anna Wohlin described as *'a lovely lady with a big heart and a great sense of humour'* (Wohlin, 2005, 245). She added *'I'm sure she loved Brian like a son, and I know that Brian loved her with all his heart. She was like a mother to him and she was someone we both depended on*. Hallett had her living-room walls bedecked with beautiful photographs and sketches of Jones and whom she would always refer to as her employer *Mr Jones*. Hallett also commented that Jones had a soft heart and that people took advantage of it (Wohlin, 2005, 176).

BRUTALITY, EXTREMETIES & VIOLENCE

Reinhart also noted that men with Chiron/Moon contacts maybe *'dominated by moodiness, emotional manipulativeness* and veiled or overt hostility towards women' (Reinhart, 1989, 196). The latter is certainly borne out by his well-known denigration and violence towards Anita Pallenberg whom he regularly beat. *'It was not unusual to see her covered in bruises, and though she was technically stronger than he, she began to worry that Brian might kill her. Friends would find Anita with black eyes, blue bruises blooming over her face and arms'* (Winder, 2023, 35), Pallenberg said that *'when the storm inside him died down he'd feel guilty and beg me to forgive him'*.

However, it wasn't just women that were subject to Jones's violence. One example being Jones's aggression towards his chauffeur Brian Palastanga, who frequently *'witnessed his chameleon-like behaviour'* (1994, Giuliano, 67). He revealed that Jones *'would be alright until he started to smoke pot, then he would change. He became violent and used to fight with people or punch a policeman'* ... Palastanga added that on one occasion he kicked him in the stomach because he wouldn't let him have the key to his Rolls Royce, presumably because Jones was drunk or stoned.

Thankfully society has progressed since the nineteen sixties. Abusive behaviour towards men and women in the UK is now recognised in law, be it emotional, financial, physical, sexual or verbal, services also exist to support those who may find themselves in an abusive relationship. Men and women who have anger management issues can also access help and this is usually through one to one counselling as well as programmes for anger management.

Astrologically It could be argued that Jones's abusive and excessive behaviour is also another illustration of the Sun square Jupiter in action and where his actions have been more than extreme and unwarranted. Bill Wyman said that the band saw in him a behaviour that *'flitted from one extreme to the other. He would not give a shit about anything and then worry about the slightest detail'* (Young, 2013, 131).

Wyman also observed that *'He could be the sweetest, softest, most considerate man in the world, or the nastiest piece of work anyone had ever met'*. Of course, this does not mean that *every* person who has the Sun square Jupiter aspect in their natal chart would behave in such extreme ways. Several years after Jones died Wyman revealed that he thought that *'Brian was a hypochondriac, a bit of a worrier; highly intelligent and very articulate'*.

Mars is conjunct Saturn and Uranus in Jones's natal chart and trine Neptune. These aspects hold some insight as to how this played out in the aforementioned areas. The contact between Mars and Uranus can symbolise potential for sexual exhilaration and sudden temper and violence. The aspect also indicates thriving on danger for excitement as well as having the urge to both generate and receive sexual satisfaction.

The Mars trine Neptune aspect denotes the possibility for sexual fantasies; this is because Mars is associated with lust and sexuality and Neptune illusion. When Pallenberg met Jones she thought he was the most sexually flexible of all *The Stones*. She commented on how Jones looked like a girl in some ways. Given that sexually she liked both men and women, Jones seemed to combine the two sexes for her. Apparently, on one occasion Jones asked her to dress him up like the French singer Françoise Hardy to which Pallenberg obliged.

She and Jones took one of the drugs of the sixties, LSD, and it became a crucial part of their sex lives. Pallenberg claimed that it gave them both great sexual freedom *'and allowed them to indulge in sexual fantasies they had suppressed: Brian's latent femininity and Anita's need for sexual dominance'* (Hotchner, 1990, 192).

Dave Thompson who lived with Jones for a short while revealed how Pallenberg was reportedly into S & M (Sadomasochism) *'I heard her going into their room with a bloody great whip. I could hear her whipping Brian'* (Giuliano, 1994, 47). The Mars Saturn conjunction can indicate (amongst other subjects) assertion with control, aggressive domination as well as being aroused and getting into the most shocking rages, releasing it only when it is safe to do so.

On another occasion when they were in Marrakesh and by themselves, Pallenberg recalled how Jones upon not getting his own way over her not being a willing party to an orgy with him and two unkempt sex-workers (Hotchner, 1990, 301) *'overturned a tray full of sandwiches and cold cuts, spilling them all over the carpet ... he began to pick things up and throw them at me. He grabbed and beat me, screaming senselessly, a tornado of violence'*.

Soon after this she left Jones for Keith Richards and she described how she *'was terrified but exhilarated to be freeing myself from Brian's tyranny'*. The emotional, physical and sexual abuse that she endured from Jones over a substantial period of time must have affected her deeply. His need to have control and power over her was endless but she finally found the courage to leave him. Paradoxically she was still intrigued by the *'good side of Brian ... the way he was when he wasn't being paranoid but I was more than ready to give that up'*.

Linda Lawrence also experienced the wrath of Jones's physical abuse. For example, he was unable to contain his jealousy of her male friends and on one occasion when they were at a party, he became thoroughly incensed and gave her a black eye. They told her parents that she had walked into a door (Wyman & Havers, 2002, 104). After Jones had left Lawrence, her mother and father discovered that he had beaten their daughter quite often (Hotchner, 1990, 126). Upon reflection Lawrence commented *'I never felt he was cruel … but rather releasing something hurtful from his past that made him angry'* (Giuliano, 1994, 27).

Nico biographer, Jennifer Otter Bickerdike revealed in explicit detail how Jones violated and sexually assaulted Nico on several occasions (Otter Bickerdike, 2022, 71). It also claimed *'The illicit substances also hampered his sexual performance, making him impotent and violent'*. Yet at other times Jones would totally desire and idolise the women. Nico said of Jones *'He was sexy. He seduced girls He was charming, until he locked the door'*. This also confirms some of Melanie Reinhart's observations and is borne out by Jones's extremities towards some of the women in his life and *'points to the wounding situations in his early relationship with his mother'* (Reinhart, 1989, 196).

Jones was on trial for drug possession two years after his affair with Nico, A psychiatric report on him was provided which said *'Mr. Jones' sexual problems are closely interrelated to his difficulties of aggression … He is still very involved with Oedipal fixations. He is very confused about the maternal and paternal role in these'*. The report continued *'Part of his confusion would seem to be the very strong resentment he* experiences toward his dominant and controlling mother, who rejected him and blatantly favoured his sister' (Otter Bikerdike, 2022, 409).

Neurologist and founder of psychoanalysis Sigmund Freud introduced the concept of the Oedipus Complex in the late eighteen eighties. However, in the context of the prevailing theories of the time when Jones's psychiatric report was produced, it suggests that Jones was afraid of repercussions from his dominant mother who would not allow his father to take a governing position.

One domestic example of this can be seen by the following situation. Linda Lawrence observed how on one occasion when she and Jones were visiting his parents. 'We walked in the house and it was as if Brian wasn't there. There was no voice or word between them. His father was a little warmer. He did react a little. Mr Jones talked and got excited but then the mother kept trying to cool him' (Aftel, 1983, 59). This demonstrates Mrs Jones domination and her husband lacking potency. Girlfriend in 1960 Pat Andrews commented on Mrs Jones stating that she was *'sure that she loved Brian she just didn't know how'* (Broomfield, 2023, Magnolia Pictures).

Linda Lawrence and Jones visited his parents at the family home several times; she recalled how his parents were *'straight and empty'* (Aftel, 1983, 59). When she met Jones's sister Barbara, she found her pleasant and *'a very straight, normal person'* who wanted to be a schoolteacher (following in the steps of her paternal grandparents). Lawrence concluded *'She was perfect for the parents – they loved her; she did everything right. Brian was probably jealous of her because she was doing everything they wanted'*. Lawrence added *'He never spoke much of her. She was perfect and went to church every Sunday'*.

BELIEF, FAITH & MORALITY

Barbara Jones being religious and a church-goer was in keeping with the Jones family heritage, she was following the family lineage in this way. Her brother attended church when he was younger to sing in the church choir (although it was unlikely that he was religious) and his father led the choir at the local church in Cheltenham. His maternal grandfather was also a church organist in Cardiff (Aftel, 1983, 59). Pat Andrews observed of Mrs Jones that *'she was a straight Baptist ... rigid ... no fun no laughter'* (Broomfield, 2023, Magnolia Pictures).

We can see a musical connection in the family through the organists and obviously Jones inherited some of this family talent.' The Sagittarius IC in Jones's natal chart is an indicator that church and religion were in the roots of his family. However, he may well have seen it as being dogmatic, moralistic and preachy as these are some of the characteristics also associated with Sagittarius.

THE MOON'S NODES AND REINCARNATION

As discussed earlier, Jones had an interest in Tibetan Buddhism, part of that spiritual practice includes the teaching that we have all lived in other incarnations. Given Jones also had some knowledge of astrology he may (or may not) have known about the concept of past-lives which can be interpreted from a natal chart. This can be interpreted through the north and south Moon nodes (also known as the Dragon's Head and the Dragon's Tail).

By deciphering the Moon's nodes (*see glossary*) using the house, sign and aspect (s) one is able to glimmer an overview of a prior life which is symbolised by the South node and indicates areas which were unresolved from that previous incarnation. The north node brings possible projections into the current life from the former life offering guidance as to how the individual can progress on their spiritual path in their exiting carnation.

In Jones's natal chart the South Node is in Pisces in the seventh house and is square to Jupiter whilst the north node is in Virgo in the first house and is also square to Jupiter. The soul-purpose of what Jones came to do in this lifetime is symbolised by the north node positioned in Virgo in the first house.

The earth element rules Virgo, the message suggesting that Jones needed to become grounded as well as finding a practical role, where he could be skilled at something particular so that it could be used by other people. Attention to the minutia of his tasks and executing them proficiently and where the detail of his skill was evident. One obvious example of how he did play out this role was his ability to bring intrinsic detail to his musicianship which counted greatly for the distinct sound of the early sound of *The Stones*. He also taught other musicians how to play in certain keys to attain an exact sound as discussed earlier. Astrologer and author Victor Olliver observed that for those with the north node in Virgo that *'Life now requires applying great ideas and principles to the tests of rigour and critique. Feet must be placed on the ground'* (Olliver, 2022, 48).

Positioned in the first house the north node has been observed by astrologer and author Steven Forrest as being the point where the person is seeking an *'enlightened selfishness'* (Forrest, 2012, 130). He continued that in relationships *'the aim is to be separate souls, on separate journeys ... Sometimes two people need different experiences ... The fear must be taken out of separation'*.

Forrest suggests that when the Moon's south node is in the seventh house the person may have taken their identity from the context of a relationship (Forrest, 2012, 129). This was borne out to a degree in the example of Jones's relationship with Pallenberg which was discussed earlier; it could be argued that this was a 'residue issue' from a former life of Jones's.

He continued that the position of the south node in the seventh house was not only confined to significant partnerships, where one may have become powerless or voiceless, but also with other one to one relationships where there are uneven balances of power. He uses the example of a client being defined by a psychotherapist. Jones as we know received therapy from psychiatrists, councillors and psychotherapists several times in his short life time.

For a person with the south node in Pisces it is a position that suggests that they have an intuitive understanding of the mysteries of life, especially those understandings which show an individual's true essence is that which goes beyond the physical. In other words, their spiritual self.

It is possible therefore that part of Jones's former life may have included being involved in spiritual practices such as fasting, meditation and devotional ritual all areas associated with Pisces. In doing so he would have sacrificed his ego and experienced a loss of the self. If he did practice the aforementioned spiritual discipline, it would have increased his psychic sensitivity and spiritual awareness as well as enhancing a tremendous faculty for creativity and imagination.

Jupiter is square to the South Node and suggests that other unresolved issues may have included yearning for fame, money and power as well as to be taken seriously and noticed. It may have been that in a former incarnation Jones saw others have these things which were then out of his reach. In this lifetime it appears that he brought with him the craving and yearning for success and the need to be applauded and noticed coupled with a total belief and faith in himself that he would achieve it.

Whether one believes in reincarnation, or not, Jones achieved his north node Virgo soul-purpose of acquiring and sharing his unique skills and being of practical help to others through his musicianship. His crave for fame and success he achieved, sadly it was short-lived due to his untimely death at the age of twenty-seven. Who knows what else he may have gone on to accomplish and create had he lived for many more years in his 1942 incarnation?

AFTERMATH & REFLECTION

Speaking after his son's death Lewis Jones felt that his son's rebuff of the university education and the professional career that he had in mind for him was at the heart of the friction between them for he stated *'The problem between Brian and myself was not so much one of personality as ambition'* (Aftel, 1982, 22). Mr Jones also said that *'Brian exasperated me beyond measure in his younger days, but my wife and I never ceased to love him'.* It is terribly sad that their son apparently never felt this affection from his parents. These comments hint that there may have been other challenges and issues at play aside from Jones's career choice.

Certainly, as an adult Jones wanted to be close to his father but not on his father's terms and even after he found success with *The Rolling Stones,* he was still seeking his approval (Aftel, 1982, 23). Keith Richards recalled how Jones would pen endless letters to his parents writing and rewriting them and even after returning from visits to his parent's home he *'would always say how he couldn't communicate with them'.* Richards concluded that out of all *The Rolling Stones 'Brian was a lot more conscious of his background and what his family thought of him than the rest of us'.*

After his son's death Lewis Jones said *'One must always look for some sign of a silver lining in whatever cloud one is presented with. And one of these silver linings has been the enormous affection in which Brian was held, not only in this country, but throughout the world'* (Jackson, 227).

PART THREE

Significant Natal & Transit Charts

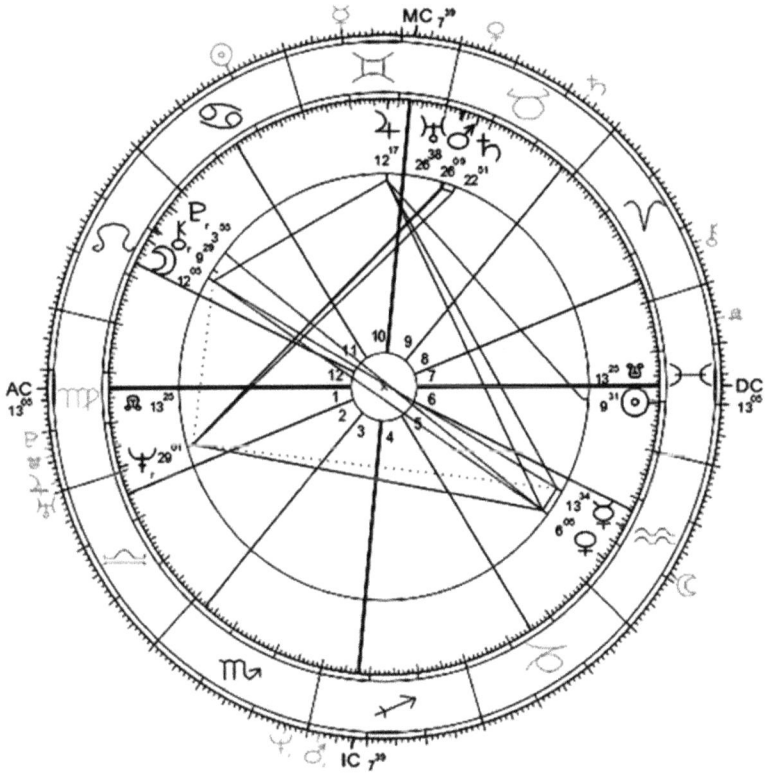

Fig. 1. Brian Jones's Natal Chart and the transits to it on the day he died – 2rd July, 1969.

The Coroner's report gave the date of Jones's death as being the 2nd July 1969 and the time of death between 11pm and 12 midnight 3rd July 1969. For astrological purposes, the date of 2nd July 1969 has been used to evaluate the astrological transits that were happening at the time of Jones's death.

Some of the major transits that Jones was having on the day he died included: transiting Jupiter in the first house conjunct natal Neptune, transiting Uranus in the first house conjunct natal Neptune, transiting Pluto in the first house trine natal Saturn, transiting Neptune in the third house opposite natal Mars and transiting Neptune in the third house opposite natal Uranus. Transiting Jupiter, Uranus and Pluto in the first house is significant given that the first house is about the self, whilst Jupiter is associated with fame and grandiose, Uranus with accidents and shock and Pluto with betrayal, death, investigation as well as, forensics and secrecy. Both Pluto and Saturn are planets associated with cycles so in terms of life and death it symbolises beginnings and endings. They are also associated with power and authorities respectively.

Transiting Neptune in the third house which is associated with communication is interesting. This is because the nature of Neptune can be vague and uncertain which alludes to the conclusion of 'misadventure'. At the inquisition this was given as the cause of death which was from drowning under the influence of alcohol and drugs whilst swimming (Giulliano, 1994, 254). The latter areas here are all associated with Neptune.

Here we can see some of the aforementioned Pluto correspondences at play here. The forensic pathologist Cyril H. Wecht was interviewed by Geoffrey Giuliano author of *Paint It Black, The Murder of Brian Jones*. The former generated an opinion as to the nature of Jones's death based on the contents and scientific data found in the documents related to the musician's death.

Some of the important points that Wecht concluded was that on the night he died, Jones was not drunk (although he had a drink) he had a high tolerance for alcohol and the effect of the alcohol would have been minimal. Another key factor was that at the time of Jones's death the only drugs found in his body was in his urine. This is significant because by the time a drug has broken down and has entered the urine, it is impossible for the substance to have any effect at all on the person (Giuliano, 1994, 167) therefore Jones was not high on drugs and neither was he drunk. One of the documents that helped Dr. Wecht reach these findings was a lab report dated 7th July 1969 made over the phone by a Mr Cook who was a biochemist at the Royal Sussex Hospital in Brighton.

Addressing the issue of the *'fatty degeneration of the liver'* he said *'It's not a diagnosis of death that I would consider at all in this case'*, his reasoning was that Jones was not in a poor enough state of health and nutrition (Giuliano, 1994, 168). Wecht also deliberated on the section *'Any further remarks'* on the Notes of the Post-Mortem Examination of Lewis Brian Hopkin Jones which said *'In death from an asthmatic attack, lungs are light and bulky'* as well as in a different part of the form where it said *'mucous associated with death due to an asthmatic attack'* (Giuliano, 1994, 252/253).

He didn't find any evidence to what was reported as to Jones having had an acute asthmatic attack. He pointed out that Jones was an accomplished swimmer and that given he was not under the influence of drugs, even if he had suffered an asthma attack whilst in the swimming pool, he would easily have been able in three or four strokes been able to swim to the other side of the pool and climb out. He added that '*an asthma attack doesn't wipe you out like a massive stroke or a large heart attack*' (Giuliano, 1994, 169).

A statement in the post-mortem says there was no overt evidence of violence that was apparent on Jones's body (Giuliano, 1994, 170). Wecht pointed out that if there is a situation where someone can be pulled under the water and it can be done without inflicting injuries to the person '*it's a diabolically clever way to kill somebody*'. He added that if one was performing an autopsy on a person that has drowned and that person has been held by two or three people so that the person cannot struggle, one could not look at the body and say the person was homicidally drowned.

The section called *The Official Documents* in Giuliano's *Paint it Black* has images of Jones's death certificate, Notes of the Post-Mortem Examination, Pathological Report, Inquisition Record, Notes from a Pathological Laboratory and details of the Deceased's Prescribed medication.

Getting back to the transits that were happening on the day that Jones died. Regarding the transiting Neptune opposition to the natal Mars aspect it indicates the following. Mars represents the 'I' act and governs the action we take when we express the needs of our Sun sign. Therefore, it could be argued that Jones had become more spiritual and less carnal when this transit was occurring. His idea of 'action' may have been forced to change. The transiting Neptune will have brought an insidious energy to the natal Mars, slowly and subtly drawing his lustful and sexual energy away.

The transit may also have resulted in Jones being more disorganised and forgetful than usual; such are some of the qualities associated with Neptune. The positive inspiring nature of Neptune would have provided him with creativity and dreams for the future as well as independence, hence for example his vision to create a new band and playing different types of music.

Another example of future wishes included marrying Anna Wohlin, starting a family with her and imagining that they had a daughter, Jones even named the girl Johanna. He even went as far as declaring excitedly to Wohlin that he wanted to make a bed himself for the child.

He decided to create a nursery for the imagined child, he started to paint the room having mixed the colour himself and calling the shade *Moroccan blue'*. He told Wohlin *'This is going to be her room. I want her to see this beautiful blue colour when she wakes up in the morning'* ... he added *'Let's paint and dream'*. These examples show how Jones was enthusiastic about the future, becoming a parent and his zest for life was apparent. He continued to talk about marriage and said that he wanted a family to take care of and to come home to (Wohlin, 2005, 164).

Wohlin stated that Jones said *'I'm longing for the day when someone crawls up into the bed and wakes me up early in the morning and says "Dad! Dad! Wake up! I want to show you something!" just like I did when I was a kid'*. This reveals that when Jones was a very young child that he then had an affectionate and warm relationship with his father if not with his mother.

Transiting Neptune in opposition to natal Uranus is a generational aspect and therefore the behaviour of Jones's age group would have experienced a changing of the times. It has been said many times that the death of Jones in 1969 indicated not only the end of the *Rolling Stones* as he had created them but also the end of an era that was paving the way for progress. Some examples of this in the 1970s include the Vietnam War ending; campaigning for equal rights for women as well as the beginning of the digital revolution.

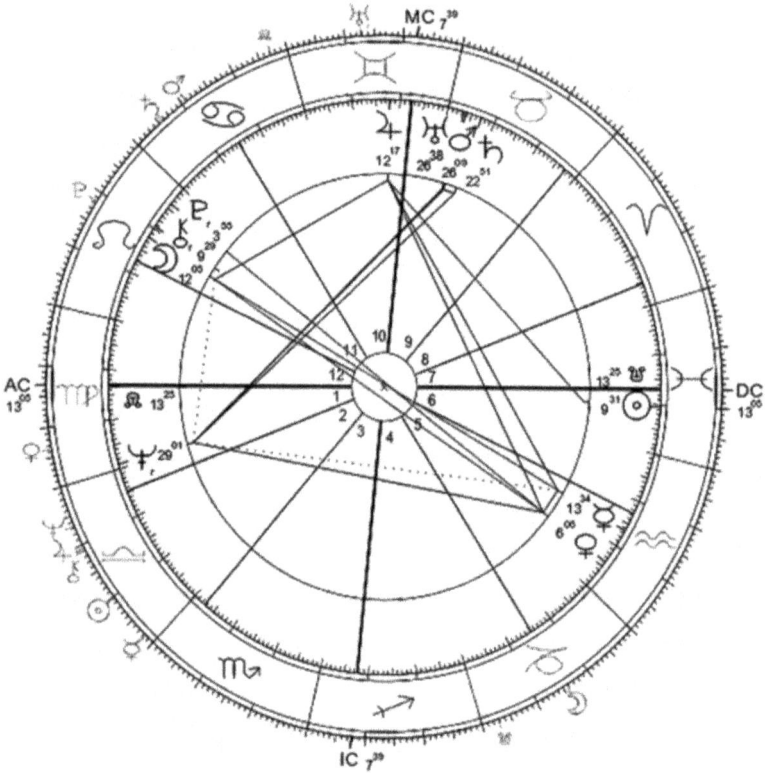

Fig. 2. The day that Jones's sister Pamela died 14th October 1945 and the transits that were being made to his natal chart on that day.

On 14th October 1945 transiting Pluto was in the eleventh house and conjunct Jones's natal Moon and natal Chiron. Associations of Pluto include: crisis, death, intensity and devastation. The eleventh house is connected with the future, goals, kindred spirits and rebellion.

SIGNIFICANT NATAL & TRANSIT CHARTS

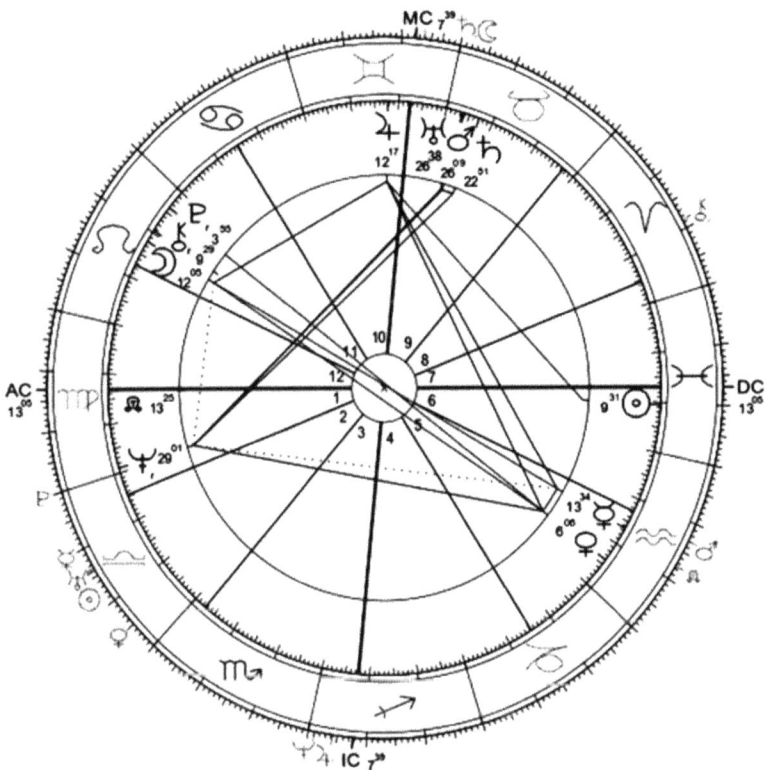

Fig. 3. The day the *Brian Jones Presents The Pipes of Pan at Jajouka* album was released on 8th October 1971 and the transits happening to Jones natal chart on that day.

When the *Brian Jones Presents The Pipes of Pan at Jajouka* album was released on 8th October 1971, had he been alive Jones would have been experiencing his second Saturn return at the ninth house. This indicates him as an established and matured musician in his own right and recognised for the ethic and different cultures he brought to music by broadening his horizons and working with different groups and music genres. Saturn is associated with challenges and so it is unsurprising perhaps that the Rolling Stones management were slow in getting the album released.

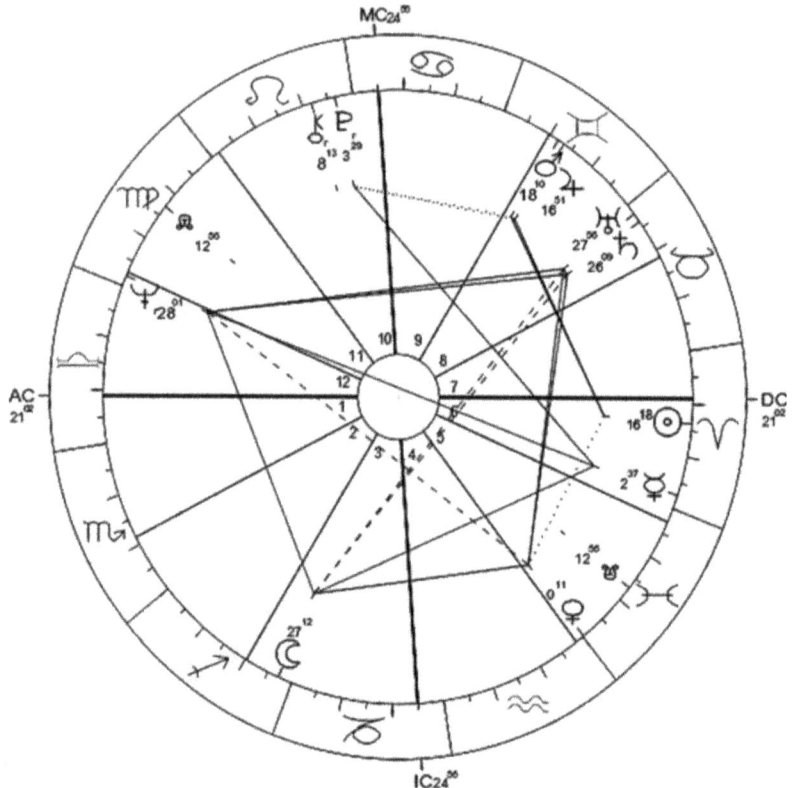

Fig. 4. Natal chart for Anita Pallenberg. Pallenberg was born on 6th April 1942 in Rome, Italy at 8.00pm.

Her natal chart shows that her Sun is in the sixth house and Venus in the fifth house which are the same positions as in Jones's natal chart. Mars, Jupiter, Uranus and Saturn are in the eighth and Neptune is in the twelfth house. It suggests an interest and fascination with the occult and other people's resources as well as witchcraft, these areas are connected with the aforementioned houses respectively. In 1985 she told author Victoria Balfour that she was not a practicing black witch and that at one time she was *'messed up about it'*. At the time she was interviewed by Balfour she admitted that she was happy to just be reading about the subject and also that she did *'believe in forces'* (Balfour, 1986, 113). Anita Pallenberg died on 13th June 2017 in Chichester; West Sussex aged seventy five years.

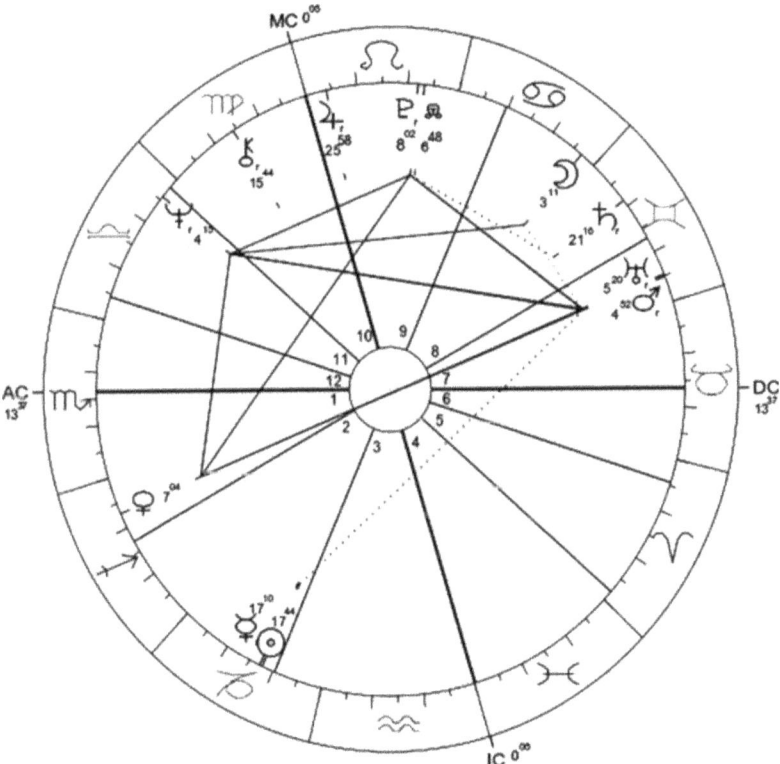

Fig. 5. Natal chart for Jimmy Page. Page was born on 9th January 1944 in Heston, Middlesex at 4.00am.

His natal chart shows a Scorpio ascendant, Moon and Saturn in the eighth house and Jupiter and Pluto in the ninth house which suggests a smouldering and mysterious persona as well as interest in the occult and enjoyment of metaphysics and philosophies.

Acknowledgments, credits & references

Prince Stash Klowosski de Rola, close friend to Brian Jones for giving me his time and sharing with me his memories from the nineteen sixties and beyond as well as answering my questions and making suggestions, invaluable.

Bill Wyman & Richard Havers for the memories, brilliant and extensive archives, research and photos which appear in *Rolling with the Stones* which have been exceptionally helpful for this project. Enormous gratitude for the masterpiece of work.

Geoffrey Giuliano, author and researcher for his ingenuous research that formed his book *Paint It Black* and which I have referred to in this book.

Frank Clifford for sharing with me the time of birth for Anita Pallenberg, the data originally obtained by astrologer and data researcher Grazia Bordoni who collected the data from the birth registry.

Andrew Jenkins for invaluable conversations about Brian Jones as well as his knowledge and wisdom on attachment and trauma.

Admin at Gloucester Nylon Spinners Facebook Group for information from some of it's members about Brian Jones working for the company.

ACKNOWLEDGMENTS, CREDITS & REFERENCES

ASTROLOGY DETAILS:

Natal and transit charts generated by www.astro.com (Astrodienst).
Rodden Rating Classification is 'C' for Brian Jones' natal chart.
Co-ordinates of Brian Jones's natal chart: 51n542w04.
Rodden Rating is 'A' for Jimmy Pages' natal chart.
Co-ordinates of Jimmy Page's natal chart: 0w22, 51n29
Rodden Rating Classification is 'AA' for Anita Pallenberg's natal chart.
Co-ordinates of Anita Pallenberg's natal chart are: 12e29, 41n54.

Birth certificate for Lewis Brian Hopkins Jones born on 28/02/1942: England and Wales, Civil Registration Birth Index 1916–207, Volume no. 6a, Page no.884. Cheltenham, Gloucestershire.

Marriage certificate for Lewis B. Jones to Louisa B. Simmonds registration date 1940: England and Wales, Civil Registration Marriage Index, 1916–2005, Marriage Index, 1916–2005, Volume no. 11a, page no. 213. Registered district: Bridgend, Inferred County: Glamorganshire.

Published copies of official documents published in *Paint It Black* by Geoffrey Guiliano 1994:
Image of Certified Copy of Lewis Brian Jones Death Certificate.
Image copy of Notes of the Post-Mortem Examination of Lewis Brian Jones from Queen Victoria Hospital in East Grinstead.

Books

Aftel, M. (1983) *Death of A Rolling Stone, The Brian Jones Story* Sidgwick & Jackson London.
Balfour, V. (1986) *Rock Wives* Beech Tree Books William Morrow.
Bickerdike Otter, J. (2022) *You Are Beautiful And You Are Alone: The Biography of Nico* Faber & Faber Limited.
Booth, S. (2012) *The True Adventures of The Rolling Stones* Cannongate Books.
Carrington, H. (1975) *Your Psychic Powers and How to Develop Them* Newcastle Publishing Co Inc.
Cooper, A. & James, D. (2020) *Brian Jones Butterfly in The Park* by New Galleon, an imprint of Genius Book Publishing.
Clifford, Frank C. (2016) *The Midheaven, Spotlight on Success* Flare Publications & The London School of Astrology.
Dalton, D. and Farren, M. (1980) *Rolling Stones in Their Own Words* Omnibus Press (a division of Book Sales Limited).
Davis, S. (2002) *Old Gods Almost Dead, The 40-Year Odyssey of The Rolling Stones.*
Dumaurier, F. (2023) *Giorgio Gomelsky 'For Your Love'* Supernova Books.
Embleton, T. (2022) *Touring and Mental Health, The Music Industry Manual* Omnibus Press.
Faithfull, M. with Dalton, D. (1995) *Faithfull* Penguin Books published by the Penguin Group.
Fitzgerald, N. (1985) *Brian Jones The Inside Story of The Original Rolling Stone* G.P. Putnam's Sons.

BOOKS

Forrest, S. (2012) *Yesterday's Sky, Astrology & Reincarnation* Seven Paws Press, Inc.

Giuliano, G. (1994) *Paint It Black. The Murder of Brian Jones* Virgin Books an imprint of Virgin Publishing Ltd.

Herman, G. (1982) *Rock 'n' Roll Babylon* Plexus, London.

Houghton, R. (2015) *You Had to Be There, The Rolling Stones Live 1962–69* Gotta Have Books.

Howard, P. (2017) *I Read the News Today, Oh Boy: The short and gilded life of Tara Browne, the man who inspired The Beatles' greatest song'* Picador an imprint of Pan Macmillan.

Hotchner, A.E. (1990) *Blown Away The Rolling Stones and The Death of The Sixties* Simon & Schuster.

Jackson, L. (1992) *Golden Stone, The Untold Life and Mysterious Death of Brian Jones* Smith Gryphon Limited.

Johns, G. (2014) *Glyn Johns Sound Man* PLUME an imprint of Penguin Random House LLC.

Mayall, J. with **McIver, J.** (2019) *Blues from Laurel Canyon, My Life As A Bluesman* Omnibus Press.

Kaldera, R. (2011) *Moon Phase Astrology, The Lunar Key To Your Destiny*.

Mitchell, M. & Platt, J. (1993) The *Hendrix Experience* Mitchell Beazley an imprint of Reed Consumer Books Ltd.

Olliver, V. (2022) *Chasing the Dragons, An Introduction to Draconic Astrology* The Wessex Astrologer Ltd.

Palmer, R (1984) *The Rolling Stones* Sphere Books Limited.

Pilcher, N. (2020) *Bent Coppers* Clink Street Publishers.

Reed, J. (1999) *Brian Jones The Last Decadent* Creation Books.

Reinhart, M. (1989) *Chiron and the Healing Journey* Arkana Penguin.

Ridder-Patrick, J. (1990) *A Handbook of Medical Astrology* Arkana Penguin.

Salewicz, C. (2018) *Jimmy Page The Definitive Biography* HarperCollins publishers.

Sasportas, H. (1985) *The Twelve Houses, An Introduction to The Houses In Astrological Interpretation* The Aquarian Press.

Sellar, W. (2008) *Introduction to Medical Astrology* The Wessex Astrologer.

Spence, S. (2021) *ALL OR NOTHING THE AUTHORISED STORY OF STEVE MARRIOTT.* Omnibus Press (a division of the Wise Music Group).

Sutton, D. (2007) *Islamic Design A Genius For Geometry* Wooden Books Ltd.

Tompkins, S. (1989) *Aspects In Astrology, A Comprehensive Guide To Interpretation* Element Books Limited.

Trynka, P. (2014) *Sympathy For The Devil The birth of the ROLLING STONES and the death of Brian Jones.* Bantam Press an imprint of Transworld Publishers.

Vyner, H. (2016) *Groovy Bob The Life & Times of Robert Fraser* HENI publishing.

Wells, S. (2021) *She's A Rainbow The Extraordinary Life of Anita Pallenberg* Omnibus Press (a division of the Wise Music Group).

Winder, E. *Parachute Women* (2023) Hachette Book Group.

Wohlin, A. (2005) *The Wild and Wicked World of Brian Jones, The True Story of My Love Affair with the Rolling Stone* Blake Publishing Ltd.

Wyman, B. with Coleman, R. (1997) *Stone Alone The Story of a Rock 'n' Roll Band* Da Capo Press.

Wyman, B. with Havers, R. (2002) *Rolling with the Stones* Dorling Kindersley.

Young, D.R. (2013) *A Memoir, Not Fade Away* Keywords Publishing.

CD Album: *Brian Jones Presents the Pipes of Pan At Jajouka* 1995 POINT music a joint venture of Euphorbia Productions Ltd. And Philips Classic Productions. All music composed and performed by The Master Musicians of Jajouka, Produced by Brian Jones.

DOCUMENTARY

The Stones and Brian Jones, (2023), Director and Co-writer Nick Broomfield, Magnolia Pictures aired in 2023 forthe BBC ontheir arts strand *Arena.*

DVD: *The Rolling Stones: Charlie is my Darling, Ireland 1965* Andrew Loog Oldham presents a film by Peter Whitehead (2012) Because Entertainment, Inc. /ABKCO Films.

FACEBOOK GROUPS

Dowty Group of Companies – Lewis Jones employment until the eighties.

Gloucester Nylon Spinners – employing Brian Jones.

The Ramrods@Cheltenham. – Brian Jones playing with them before he formed *The Rollin' Stones.*

Websites

https://amfmtreatment.com/valium-for anxiety/#:~:text= Valium%20(diazepam)%20is%20a%20medication, calming%20the%20brain%20and%20nerves – accessed on 23/11/2023 Valium being used to help manage seizures.

https://ancestors.familysearch.org/en/ – accessed on 15/11/2023 – Dates of birth and death for Lewis Blount Jones and Louisa Beatrice Simmonds.

https://www.astro.com/astro-databank/Jones,_Brian – accessed on 13/10/2023 – Brian Jones natal chart with time of birth.

https://www.astro.com/astro-databank/Monroe,_Marilyn – accessed on 13/10/2023 – natal chart showing Neptune in the first house.

https://www.asthmaandlung.org.uk/ – accessed on 25/07/2023.

https://www.beatlesbible.com/people/george-harrison/songs/pisces-fish/ – accessed on 14/10/2023 – *Pisces Fish* lyrics Pisces themes and symbolism – written by George Harrison and produced by Dhani and George Harrison and Jeff Lynne.

http://brianjonesblues.co.uk/ – accessed on 13/12/2023. – Diddley quote about trying to pull the group ahead.

https://www.christies.com/en/lot/lot-3902546 – accessed on 21/09/2023 – Lot essay with extract from Marianne Faithfull's autobiography describing Ruby Tuesday as being Brian Jones 'swan song'.

WEBSITES

- https://www.classicbands.com/BarbaraAnneMarion Interview.html – accessed on 09/09/2023 interview with Gary James and Barbara Anna Marion, daughter of Brian Jones.
- https://www.collinsdictionary.com/dictionary/english/satyriasis – accessed on 05/01/2024 – definition of satyriasis.
- https://www.dowtyheritage.org.uk/ – accessed on 30/08/'23 – leading British manufacturer information.
- https://www.denofgeek.com/culture/the-rolling-stones-and-the-mystery-of-brian-jones-death/ – accessed on 09/09/2023 – The Roosters band formed with Paul Jones.
- https://en-academic.com/dic.nsf/enwiki/6173040 – accessed on 22/12/2023 – Suki Poitier and Robert Ho's final hours.
- https://en.wikipedia.org/wiki/Brian_Jones – accessed on 06/09/2023 – musicians he formed friendships with when he first came to London.
- https://en.wikipedia.org/wiki/Brian_Jones – accessed on 13/09/2023 – detail of musical instruments Jones played.
- https://en.wikipedia.org/wiki/Brian_Jones#CITEREFJagger RichardsWattsWood2003 – accessed on 10/09/2023 – the band became *The Rollin' Stones*.
- https://en.wikipedia.org/wiki/Zouzou_ (model) – accessed on 06/09/2023 – lead role in film and introduction to Brian Jones in Paris.
- https://en.wikipedia.org/wiki/Brian_Jones – accessed on 19/09/'23 – excesses in life leading to the detriment of Jones's mental and physical health.
- https://en.wikipedia.org/wiki/Brian_Jones – accessed on 21/09/'23 – in no fit condition to tour in 1969.

WEBSITES

https://en.wikipedia.org/wiki/Brian_Jones – accessed on 21/09/2023 – Jones took the band's Jaguar to go shopping it was towed away,

https://en.wikipedia.org/wiki/Brian_Jones – accessed on 21/09/2023 – ones crashing his motorbike and having to go to hospital.

https://en.wikipedia.org/wiki/Degree_of_Murder – accessed on 22/09/2023 – details of the film 'A Degree of Murder' along with creatives.

https://en.wikipedia.org/wiki/The_Brian_Jonestown_Massacre#:~:text=The%20band%20name%20is%20a,followers%20died%20in%20a%20mass – accessed on 27/11/2023.

https://en.wikipedia.org/wiki/The_Master_Musicians_of_Joujouka – accessed on 23/09/2023 – trance musicians-brought to international attention by Jones.

https://en.wikipedia.org/wiki/Brian_Jones – accessed on 23/09/2023 – Master Musicians of Morocco – H & B Attar.

https://en.wikipedia.org/wiki/Robert_Fraser_ (art dealer) – accessed on 03/01/2024 six months hard labour in HM Wormwood Scrubs.

https://en.wikipedia.org/wiki/Volker_Schl%C3%B6ndorff – accessed on 23/09/2023. – Volker Schlöndorff – New German Cinema.

https://en.wikipedia.org/wiki/All_Along_the_Watchtower – accessed on 23/09/2023 – Vibraslap percussion instrument – Bob Dylan wrote *Watchtower* Jones played on *Watchtower* for *The Jimi Hendrix Experience*.

https://www.freebmd.org.uk/cgi/information.pl?r=224282526:6792&d=bmd_1689976433 – accessed on 02/09/2023 details of Julian Mark Andrews's birth.

WEBSITES

https://www.marieclaire.com/fashion/g2164/supermodels-of-the-60s/ – accessed on 09/09/2023 – Donyale Luna overdose.

https://peopleshistorynhs.org/encyclopaedia/birth-control-on-the-nhs/ – accessed on 08/10/2023 – Birth Control and the Contraceptive Pill.

https://www.release.org.uk/about# – accessed on 15/12/2023 – information about their mission and when they were founded. Charity number:801118.

https://www.bbc.co.uk/religion/religions/buddhism/subdivisions/tibetan_1.shtml – accessed on 31/01/2024 – visual aids used in Tibetan Buddhism.

https://www.reuters.com/article/us-jones-idUSTRE58E0KP20090915/ – accessed on 19/11/2023 – Los Angeles Reuters *'New suspect emerges in possible Brian Jones murder'*.

https://rollingstones.com/tour/ accessed on 24/12/2023 – Hackney Diamonds tour 2024.

https://www.shadyoldlady.com/location/2645 – accessed on 28/12/2023 – Jimmy Page's Equinox.

https://www.stonewall.org.uk/about-us/news/short-history-word-bisexuality – accessed on 21/12/2023.

https://www.wherecanwego.com/item/e408994/the-ramrods – accessed on 23/09/2023 – gave Jones his first break before forming *The Rollin' Stones*.

youtube Films

https://www.youtube.com/watch?v=JcNXmkyYjDw
  Brian Jones Rare Interview re: his thoughts on marriage (see also reference for DVD *The Rolling Stones Charlie is my Darling*).

https://www.youtube.com/watch?v=j8OANZg8_iE
  Pat Andrews With Her Son Mark (Brian Jones was the father) (circa 1964).

https://www.youtube.com/watch?v=LdY8zmuGJjI
  Brian Jones on the Generation Gap (New Audio) (Rolling Stones Documentary.

https://www.youtube.com/watch?v=R9onQIxrlno-
  Wondery – British Scandal – Matt Ford and Alice Levine, *Death of A Rolling Stone:* interview Prince Stash (Stanislas Klossowski de Rola) friend of Brian Jones – accessed on 11/12/2023.

https://www.youtube.com/watch?v=Klx-IDQEwy4-
  yogaCast – accessed on 06/01/2024- Brian Jones meets Maharishi Makesh Yogi.

Glossary of Terms

Angle: the angles in an astrological chart are the four cardinal points which comprise of; The Ascendant, the Midheaven, the Descendant and the Imum Coeli.

Ascendant: the sign of the Zodiac ascending at the time of one's birth on the eastern horizon it is also known as the Rising Sign.

Aspect: is an angle the planets make to each other in the horoscope, as well as with the Ascendant, Midheaven, Descendant and Lower Heaven (IC).

Astrology: is the study of the influence that planets have on human lives.

Axis: the areas on a Natal chart where the Ascendant, MC, Descendant and IC are situated are also known as the 'angles'.

Chiron: is an asteroid and in astrology symbolises the 'Wounded Healer', it represents our deepest wounds and endeavours to heal it. Chiron orbits the Sun between Saturn and Uranus.

Clairaudience: the faculty or power of hearing something not present to the ear but regarded as having objective reality.

Clairvoyance: means 'clear-seeing' and is a type of psychic gift, which allows the psychic to see the hidden.

Co-ordinates: for place birth of birth show the degrees and minutes for the *place* of birth (longitude and latitude).

Correspondences: associations, links.

GLOSSARY OF TERMS

Critical Degrees: the degrees of 0 and 29 in a sign, they are critical because they are the first and final degree.

Descendant: the Descendant is the cusp of the seventh house.

Glyphs: are symbols that astrologers use for the planets, signs, asteroids and other points in an astrological chart.

Hard Aspect: refers to major angles created between planets, which comprise of the opposition, square and sometimes the conjunction (n.b. the latter is variable depending on the energies of the two planets involved).

Houses: a house in the natal chart reveal 'where' planetary energies express themselves. Each of the twelve houses in a chart, rule certain areas of life, types of people and relationships, ideas and circumstances of life.

Imum Coeli/IC: Coeli is Latin for 'Bottom of The Sky.' The Imum Coeli is the 'nadir' or low point in the Sun's path and if you could see the Sun where it would be seen at Midnight, it is also the cusp of the 4th house.

Major aspects: comprise of Conjunction, Opposition, Sextile, Square and Trine angles.

Medium: the person doing the mediumship, the channel through which spirit communicates and the medium delivers the communication.

Midheaven /MC Coeli: is Latin for heaven, Medium Coeil is the Midheaven is the where the Sun would be at noon at the top of the chart, it is also the 10th house cusp.

Modes: there are three modes in astrology which are represented by cardinal, fixed and mutable energies. They all represent the way in which a sign operates. **Cardinal** signs are initiators of action and are the signs of Aries, Cancer, Libra and Capricorn. **Fixed** signs have staying power and are the signs Taurus; Leo, Scorpio and Aquarius **Mutable** signs have a versatile attitude and are the signs are Gemini, Virgo, Sagittarius and Pisces.

Natal Chart: a Natal chart is a picture of the positions of the signs, planets and angles at the time of one's birth. It contains data such as date, time and place of birth to generate an accurate astrological chart.

Opposition: is a hard aspect is which creates an angle of $180°$ with another planet.

Psychic Phenomena: a type of phenomena that appears to contradict physical laws.

Rodden Rating System: a system developed by astrologer Lois Rodden which classifies astrological data by grade to reflect its accuracy for research and purposes for astrologers. Classification starts at 'AA' then 'A' and finishes at 'XX' – for further details see https://www.astro.com/astro-databank/Help:RR.

Sextile: is a soft aspect which creates an angle at $60°$ with another planet.

Soft Aspect: refers to major angles created between planets, which comprise of the conjunction; sextile and trine (n.b. the conjunction is variable depending on the energies of the two planets involved).

Square Aspect: is a planet which creates a $90°$ angle with another planet.

Tarot: a Tarot pack consists of 78 cards; divided into the Major Arcana of 22 cards and the Minor Arcana of 56 cards which are divided into 4 suits of; Wands. Coins or Pentacles and Swords and Cups. The Minor Arcana cards correspond to the 4 elements; Wands fire, Coins or

Pentacles earth, Swords air and Cups water. A Tarot deck can be used for divination and spiritual advice and self-development.

Transits: the planets continue their movement and complete their cycles, they form special relationships to the planets and points in our individual natal charts.

Trine: is a soft aspect which creates a 120° angle with another planet.

Zodiac: the Zodiac Belt is the circle around which the Sun moves month by month. It moves through the 12 constellation signs which are divided equally by 30° divisions.

Milton Keynes UK
Ingram Content Group UK Ltd.
UKHW021020080324
439153UK00011B/257